TOTAL NEEDS SELLING

FIFTH EDITION

Dearborn
R&R Newkirk
a division of Dearborn Financial Publishing, Inc.

While a great deal of care has been taken to provide accurate and current information, the ideas, suggestions, general principles and conclusions presented in this text are subject to local, state and federal laws and regulations, court cases and any revisions of same. The reader is thus urged to consult legal counsel regarding any points of law—this publication should not be used as a substitute for competent legal advice.

This text is updated periodically to reflect changes in laws and regulations. To verify that you have the most recent update, you may call Dearborn•R&R Newkirk at 1-800-423-4723 and ask for the Supervised Study Department.

©1976–1984, 1986, 1990, 1992 by Dearborn Financial Publishing, Inc.
Published by Dearborn•R&R Newkirk, a division of Dearborn Financial Publishing, Inc.

All rights reserved. The text of this publication, or any part thereof, may not be reproduced in any manner whatsoever without written permission from the publisher.

Printed in the United States of America.

Sixth printing, November 1995

Library of Congress Cataloging-in-Publication Data

Total needs selling.—5th ed.
      p. cm.
   ISBN 0-79310-431-9
   1. Insurance, Life—Agents. 2. Insurance, Life—Marketing.
3. Selling. I. Dearborn•R&R Newkirk.
HG8877.T68   1992   92-12710
368.3′2′88—dc20   CIP

⬛⬛⬛⬛⬛ Table of Contents

▪▪▪▪▪ Introduction

T his text is designed to give you a complete and practical understanding of total needs selling. Two different methods—capital utilization and capital retention—are used to provide solutions to such modern challenges as the two-income family, high interest rates and investment yields, higher benefits from government programs and inflation.

▪ ▪ ▪ ▪ ▪

The *Total Needs Selling* course is designed to provide the life insurance agent with a working knowledge of total needs selling as a marketing technique—not only for life insurance but to uncover any other insurance need as well. Whenever the agent discovers a need for life insurance, there may also be a need for disability income insurance, a better group insurance plan at work, a buy-sell agreement funded by life insurance, estate planning and business insurance needs. In short, *Total Needs Selling* can open many markets for the insurance agent.

▪ TWO METHODS

The objective of the *capital utilization* method is to solve financial needs by using scientifically liquidated capital plus earnings. Programming (the use of both capital and interest in creating life insurance settlement options) is an example of this method. The *capital retention* method is used to satisfy financial needs through earnings generated by a sufficient capital base.

Either or both of these methods can help you take that big step beyond single-need, package selling into the lucrative total needs market. You'll learn about fact-finding, engineering and selling the plan, post-sale service and finding new prospects for more sales.

■ A NEW STEP IN YOUR CAREER

As a new life insurance agent, you are prepared to pursue the total needs approach to selling if your achievements include the following:

- completion of an introductory training program and an acceptable production level;
- a thorough understanding of the basic policy structure and settlement options;
- familiarity with rate books, applications and other related forms;
- good prospecting and daily work habits and
- an organized sales procedure and the development of at least one effective sales presentation.

If you are an established life insurance agent, the total needs approach can be rewarding if you:

- recognize that continued personal growth is conducive to career advancement;
- realize that proper service to increasingly sophisticated clients and prospects with constantly changing needs requires increased knowledge and skill;
- want to set up a broader and more secure business by building a diversified clientele and
- recognize that extending your services into diverse fields can increase production and personal income.

■ STUDY PRELIMINARIES

Three preliminary steps should be taken before beginning an in-depth study of the text.

1. Scan the Table of Contents for a glimpse of the subjects you will be studying.
2. Read the brief summary provided on the first page of each chapter. It provides a broad overview of key information in the chapter.
3. Skim the *Guide to Social Security* booklet that accompanies this course. This booklet is provided solely to help explain Social Security concepts; it does not necessarily reflect current Social Security figures.

1

An Overview of Total Needs Selling

T his introduction will describe for you—the life insurance agent—what total needs selling is, why it is important, who it best serves and how it is sold. Important terms and concepts, such as the five phases of the total needs sale, are presented and defined. You will recognize the total needs approach as an excellent way to benefit yourself and your clients.

■ ■ ■ ■ ■

Many people feel that the total needs selling concept is equal in importance to the life insurance principles of legal reserves and nonforfeiture values. The total needs concept leads to more sales in larger amounts, and it has improved the public image of life insurance agents.

Total needs selling today is the basis of sound family financial counseling and continuing service. In more complex cases it is the cornerstone of estate planning. Therefore, enterprising life insurance agents should master this marketing concept and its techniques. Let's start by reviewing the what, who, why and how to help you visualize the overall picture. Later we'll examine the important details.

■ WHAT IT IS

Total needs selling is defined as *a service and marketing system designed to satisfy a family's cash and income needs if a breadwinner's earnings are cut off because of death or retirement, through one coordinated plan that includes one sale of any additional life insurance needed.*

Note that total needs selling is *designed* to satisfy all income and cash needs with *one* plan and *one* sale. However, actual practice frequently results in variations such as partially adopting the plan or totally adopting it based on periodic purchases of insurance, perhaps spread over several years. Such variations aren't necessarily bad. You often can use them in tailoring a total needs presentation to a prospect's particular situation.

Note also the two limitations to the above definition. First, death, retirement and disability are particularly significant events that could cut off a breadwinner's earnings. This text emphasizes death and retirement. Second, *any additional insurance needs* refers solely to life insurance. With these limitations in mind, let's examine the total needs definition more closely, including explanations of certain terms.

Breadwinner

The term *breadwinner* refers to a provider of income for the family. Traditionally, the husband was the primary and often the sole breadwinner of the family. Consequently, the one-income family usually was the only arrangement considered with respect to total needs selling. Wives today share the income-producing role with their husbands in more than one-half of all families, according to recent statistics. Total needs selling, therefore, also must address the wife's contribution if it significantly affects the family's standard of living and long-range financial stability. In a two-income family a total needs selling concept and technique must consider the effect of the dual income.

Some women, such as widows, divorcees and wives of disabled husbands, may be the sole producers of family income and clearly are included in the definition of breadwinner. A spouse planning to work temporarily or intermittently is not considered a breadwinner within the context of our discussion.

Service and Marketing System

Total needs selling is a combined service and marketing system. It provides a *service* by helping people recognize their current financial problems and it provides sound solutions to them. Moreover, it is a continuing service that addresses new problems and changing circumstances as they occur.

Marketing in this text means the sales distribution of life insurance. The best solutions to a family's important cash and income problems usually include the need for and purchase of additional life insurance. The very essence of total needs selling is *service* and *marketing*. It's an effective one-piece "system" that includes identifying a family's financial problems, solving those problems and then selling the most favorable solutions.

Family's Cash and Income Needs

A family's three vital uses for income are for food, clothing and shelter. However, a family also needs income if it is to pay for automobiles, vacations, medical and dental expenses, bicycles, entertainment, educations, new roofs, new televisions and stereos, emergencies and many other important needs that are part of a family's style of living. In the typical situation these needs are satisfied by the earnings of one or more breadwinners. It's probably no coincidence that the family's standard of living and income needs normally tend to exactly equal earnings. As long as the natural balance between income needs and earnings continues, no serious financial problems usually surface.

But what if a breadwinner's earnings are cut off by death or retirement? Without those earnings to meet income needs, the family's former financial balance is destroyed and a new balance, usually at a lower level, is established. For example, at a breadwinner's death, the family's *income* needs for food, clothing, shelter and other expenses are somewhat reduced. The family's other income needs continue at about the same level, however.

The breadwinner's death normally creates additional *cash* needs. These needs virtually always include cash to pay last illness and funeral costs, mortgage expenses as well as other indebtedness and probate and other estate settlement costs. They also may include federal and state death taxes and other taxes. These costs often must be paid promptly before the surviving family members can receive the remainder of the deceased breadwinner's estate.

Thus we see that a family has both *cash* and *income* needs when a breadwinner dies. These are the needs that this total needs *service and marketing system* is designed to satisfy.

A different situation exists when a breadwinner's earnings stop at retirement. The income needs continue but on a somewhat lower scale. The children usually are grown and on their own, so family income needs typically are limited to the requirements of just husband and wife. Some of these needs decrease or cease—travel to and from work, lunches, clothes, etc. Sometimes the standard of living and recreational pursuits are reduced. Moreover, mortgage payments and other debts may no longer be a factor.

Nonetheless, substantial and vital income needs do continue after a breadwinner retires. Satisfaction of those needs is the important secondary purpose of total needs selling.

One Coordinated Plan and One Sale

The system for satisfying a family's *cash* and *income needs* by total needs selling may be outlined as follows:

1. One coordinated plan:
   a. Set forth all cash and income needs of the family.
   b. Apply all cash and income that would be available from current assets and other sources, thus clearly demonstrating any deficiencies that are not offset by cash and/or income from current assets and other sources.
2. One sale:
   a. Propose additional life insurance on the breadwinner to offset any cash and/or income deficiencies revealed above.
   b. Sell that proposal.

Variations

As noted earlier, actual practice frequently results in variations. Variations arise because a prospective buyer is unable or unwilling to pay for the additional insurance needed to complete the plan as recommended. In such situations, several alternatives are available.

1. A lower-premium type of insurance, possibly covering all needs in case of death but not retirement.
2. A reduced amount of insurance with a corresponding reduction in the satisfaction of needs—usually according to the prospective buyer's priorities. This

      may range from partial satisfaction of all needs to full satisfaction of some
      needs and no satisfaction of others.

3. A current purchase of "1" or "2" above accompanied by a schedule of future conversions or purchases aimed at completing the total plan.

Another variation occurs because total needs selling is not a static process. It must be repeated periodically as the need arises. We don't want to create the impression that "one plan and one sale" provides the ideal solution to a family's financial needs forever. A family's structure, standard of living, needs, desires and income assets are all subject to change. It happens either as a result of some specific event or with the passage of time, together with inflationary changes. With each change affecting the family, the plan and insurance amount usually require adjustments.

The family's total needs must be reviewed periodically if its cash and income needs are to remain satisfied. Periodic reviews and continuing service also are important to you because they foster client-building and repeat sales.

One final variation from our definition is that *one sale* may involve the sale of more than one policy. For example, more than one type of insurance might be required to satisfy the family's needs, or insurance on more than one breadwinner might be required. Nonetheless, total needs selling is designed to do the whole job with "one sale" of all insurance needed, no matter how many policies are required.

■ WHO NEEDS IT?

Who needs total needs selling?

First, look for a family situation that includes at least one breadwinner whose earnings totally or partially meet the family's cash and income needs.

Second, the family's earnings and/or financial situation, such as current assets, should be average or above average. Although all families have needs, only those with the financial ability to pay for your recommendations are good prospects. Middle-income to upper-income families are best. Even the very well-to-do often have unresolved financial needs. At least one of the various solutions available in total needs selling is appropriate to any given situation.

Third, the breadwinner(s) must be insurable because total needs selling is based on the sale of life insurance to provide the additional cash or income needed.

Finally, as in other types of selling, an accessible and receptive family member is vital.

So in prospecting for total needs selling, look for a middle-income or better family situation with at least one healthy, insurable, accessible and receptive breadwinner.

■ WHY IT IS IMPORTANT

Why is total needs selling so highly recommended? A major attribute of total needs selling is its thorough, businesslike approach to family financial planning and the purchase of life insurance. The system is consumer-oriented. It identifies the family's important needs and employs maximum economies and utility of assets to meet them. So if families need additional life insurance, they know how much, what kind and why. They also know where to turn when they need service.

For life insurance agents, the total needs selling system has many advantages. By employing this system, you perform a professional service that builds your prestige and promotes client relationships. Moreover, because your clients have a clear understanding of their total needs, what they are buying and why, your sales usually are larger, close easier and persist better than other personal sales in family-type situations.

■ HOW IT IS SOLD

How is total needs selling accomplished? After the preliminary steps of the sales process (prospecting, approach, etc.), total needs selling moves through five phases: fact-finding, plan design, presentation, sale wrap-up and service/periodic reviews.

Fact-Finding

In this phase (also called the *data interview*), you obtain all pertinent facts about the family. Those facts include (1) personal information (ages, health, etc.); (2) vocational and avocational information; (3) financial needs, obligations, desires and goals, with an indication of priorities and (4) details about current assets and other potential sources of cash or income.

Plan Design

The next phase is designing a sound, practical, effective plan that will satisfy the family's financial needs if the breadwinner's death or retirement cuts off part or all of its income. This step first applies existing assets and other potential sources of lump-sum cash or periodic income to the family's financial needs. Then the appropriate amount and type of life insurance required to make up any cash or income deficiencies is determined.

Plan design may be done manually or by computer. It may employ either the capital utilization method or the capital retention method.

The total plan is portrayed clearly, often graphically or in balance-sheet style. It may include a formal proposal recommending purchase of the additional life insurance required to complete the plan.

Presentation

The presentation phase is the review of the plan with the prospective buyer. You outline the family's financial needs, review any deficiencies and show how far current assets will go. This sets the stage for the ideal solution—purchasing additional life insurance needed to fill the present deficits.

Sale Wrap-Up

After the sale is made, the details of completing the application, arranging for a medical exam, if needed, and submitting the case to the company are the same as for any other sale. Care must be taken in selecting beneficiaries and settlement options. In the total needs sale, however, you also assume the responsibility of helping the buyer make certain that all other policies have beneficiary and settlement directions in keeping with the plan. This usually involves handling all such necessary changes or additions, with the policyowner's authorization.

Service and Periodic Reviews

Your activities after the sale are about the same as with any type of sale. They include (1) examining the new policy for accuracy; (2) preparing the policy and a summary in a way that reaffirms the buyer's confidence in the plan and (3) following up periodically with promised plan reviews and continuing service.

Following the total needs sale, however, at least two of these activities are more extensive than during a single-need or package sale. First, a more extensive summary is prepared and delivered with the policy. It summarizes the total plan and explains the roles that the client's policies and other assets play in that plan.

Second, the pattern of periodic reviews and continuing service is much more important in total needs selling. An outdated plan might affect adversely the proper use and arrangement of all the client's assets, possibly with disastrous results for the client-agent relationship and for the family's financial well-being. For example, consider the impact of inflation alone—even if the family's situation does not change. If the cost of living has gone up, say, 5 percent per year for three years, 15 percent more capital will be needed to accomplish what was established just three years ago. If six years have passed since the total needs sale, 30 percent more capital will be needed.

Of course, the possible changes in the family's other assets and the possible changes in the family's needs or objectives during that time must be taken into consideration in determining their new total insurance needs. But the need for periodic reviews becomes especially significant when today's economy is taken into consideration.

Clearly, you'll want to be sure that the plans you design and sell are serviced properly and kept up-to-date. It's not only good business, it's a moral obligation and responsibility you take on when you make a total needs sale.

We'll move on to more detailed, in-depth examinations of those particular aspects of total needs selling that set it apart from other sale techniques.

■ CHAPTER 1 QUESTIONS FOR REVIEW

1. Cash expenses at death refer to:
   a. ongoing expenses like food, clothing and educational costs.
   b. final expenses such as doctor and funeral bills, estate settlement costs and death taxes.
   c. Both a and b
   d. Neither a nor b

2. Total needs selling is a:

   a. sales system.
   b. method of keeping track of client purchases.
   c. system for keeping track of agent sales.
   d. combined service and marketing system.

3. An outdated total needs plan could:

   a. save the agent expensive service calls on the family.
   b. force the insured to call the agent and guarantee another sale.
   c. have a disastrous impact on the family's financial well-being.
   d. mean that the agent has more important work to do than service work.

4. Total needs plans can be designed using:

   a. capital utilization.
   b. capital retention.
   c. Both a and b
   d. Neither a nor b

5. The objective of total needs fact-finding, plan design and presentation is:

   a. the sale of mortgage insurance to protect the family home.
   b. the purchase of life insurance to fill the revealed deficits.
   c. to set another appointment in six months to see if the situation has changed.
   d. None of the above

Total Needs Fact-Finding

A ccurate and thorough fact-finding is essential to the total needs sale. As you gather data and learn your prospect's objectives, you show the prospect financial problems that can be resolved through the purchase of additional life insurance. This chapter familiarizes you with a standard fact-finding form and tells you how to use it to keep the interview and sales process moving in a positive direction. A summary of total needs and a premium commitment are your objectives.

■ ■ ■ ■ ■

Fact-finding aids virtually all kinds of sales activity; however, in total needs selling, it is essential. Proper fact-finding techniques can expose a family's fundamental financial needs to the extent that the subsequent presentation and close are little more than formalities.

Total needs fact-finding obtains information that will reveal a family's financial needs and desires. Two general types of information are required:

1. *Raw facts* about the prospect and other family members—dates of birth, present insurance, assets and other statistical types of data.
2. *Personal information* about the people themselves—attitudes and values, interests, desires and aspirations.

Raw facts are required to compute rates, make recommendations, fill out applications and provide routine service. But the personal information you gather is the key to motivating the prospect.

■ FACT-FINDING OBJECTIVES

Determining what a potential buyer wants is essential to professional selling. Effective fact-finding should be more than analytical. Both the quantity of your sales and the quality of your service are directly related to the amount of personal information you obtain from prospects. Let's briefly cover the basic objectives.

Main Objectives

The main objectives of total needs fact-finding are to:

1. record all essential personal and financial data;
2. guide the prospect in setting realistic financial objectives and
3. obtain a definite commitment.

Successful life insurance agents adhere to this sequence. The progression is logical: Start with the relatively easy procedure of recording the facts, then move into the more sensitive and demanding job of evaluating personal needs and goals. During the process, you also accomplish some collateral objectives that help to bring the sale closer.

Collateral Objectives

Beyond getting raw facts, the fact-finding phase should motivate prospects to want to know more about setting financial objectives and solving financial problems. Psychologists say that motivation is a subjective process that occurs within prospects themselves. The life insurance agent merely serves as an external stimulus that keeps the process moving along, helping prospects recognize existing internal wants and desires. You help prospects to motivate themselves.

How can you accomplish this? Mainly by skillful questioning that gets prospects to talk about their personal concerns and desires. Through this process, both you and your prospects can understand their needs more fully.

Another important collateral objective of the fact-finding phase is to bring any hidden *objections* to the surface. Otherwise, during the close, your prospects may voice these objections as reasons for not buying. Such surprises can kill sales.

Finally, extensive fact-finding is the foundation of a sound client-agent relationship based on continuing service. You can tailor proposed solutions to a particular client's needs only if you know all the facts and personal information about the client's circumstances.

A good job of fact-finding likely will result in a sale, a loyal client and a number of sales in the future.

Essential Data

It's almost impossible to determine precisely how much information to obtain in the fact-finding interview. Some agents can engineer a sound plan by securing the following information about a prospect: birth date, income, family makeup (all dependents), home ownership, general information about assets and liabilities, specifics about life insurance owned, estimate of income needs and what the prospect wants to do for dependents.

Other agents obtain detailed information about virtually all aspects of the general and life insurance estates, especially for well-to-do prospects. The amount of data gathered in each fact-finding situation should depend on what you already know about your prospect through prospecting and preapproach activities. If information is too limited, you may overlook essential elements in the new plan. However, too much minor information can tempt you to develop a plan that is too intricate. It could confuse the prospect and, thus, jeopardize the sale.

■ FACT-FINDING FORMS

To maintain control during the discussion and to provide guidelines, it's best to approach the interview with a prepared fact sheet. Excellent forms are available through various publishing companies; many life insurance companies furnish data sheets to their agents. A personally prepared form is still another possibility. Some agents feel that a form prepared to their specifications makes them more effective in the fact-finding procedure.

For illustration and discussion, a sample fact-finding form, Ill. 2.1, appears on pages 11–14. Look it over. Note that the basic functions of its various parts are labeled. The *Financial Data* section is where the sources of *income*, of money coming in, are listed in detail. These are the assets the family has available.

The *Family Financial Objectives* represent money going *out*. Some of these objectives are actually fixed obligations—many of the final expenses, payments for food, clothing, housing, etc. Others may be goals for the family, such as an emergency fund, bequests or money for education. Even though they may be listed as a "goal," they are real obligations that *must* be met somehow.

Family Data

The first section of the form, shown on page 15 as Ill. 2.2, is devoted to obtaining basic personal facts about each family member and other dependents. It contains the minimum essential information for any prospect file. Because this identifying information is routine and easy to obtain, starting here helps to get the prospect's active cooperation at the outset.

Note that throughout this form, the prospect is identified as "you." This can refer to a family head of either sex or to either spouse. Asking about the prospect's health at this point tends to reveal some key qualifying information early and might save time and effort. The question concerning business ownership reveals information you'll want sooner or later. It naturally follows the questions about the prospect's occupation and place of employment.

The second section of the form has questions about the spouse and these are identical to the ones asked about the prospect. Note that the form can be used with either spouse to obtain the desired information about both, including employment data. If there is no spouse, mark this segment "NA" (not applicable) or leave it blank. The same applies to the occupational questions for a nonworking spouse. If the answer to any question is the same for both spouse and prospect (e.g., home address and telephone number) simply answer it "same."

The part *Your Children and/or Other Dependents* is also fairly routine. Record full names to help with beneficiary provisions or other purposes. Relationship, birth date, age, sex and general state of health of each dependent are all items of information that you need now or will find valuable in the future. Additional information may surface about a child—special talents, educational goals, handicaps, etc.—that may be the key to present and future sales.

ILL. 2.1 ■ Sample Fact-Finding Form

ESSENTIAL INFORMATION

This is the first step in a personalized service designed to illustrate clearly the values of your life insurance and to make your life insurance serve you most effectively. The accuracy of this service depends on the exactness of the information given. All information will be held in strict confidence.

Date _____

FAMILY DATA

YOU

Your Name: _____ Birth Date: _____ Health: _____

Home Address: _____ Home Telephone: _____

Occupation: _____ Employer: _____

Business Address: _____ Business Telephone: _____

Do you and/or your spouse own an interest in the business? _____ Details: _____

_____

(If an answer is the same as above or not applicable, write "Same" or "N.A." respectively in the blank.)

YOUR SPOUSE

Spouse's Name: _____ Marriage Date: _____ Birth Date: _____ Health: _____

Home Address: _____ Home Telephone: _____

Occupation: _____ Employer: _____

Business Address: _____ Business Telephone: _____

Do you and/or your spouse own an interest in the business? _____ Details: _____

_____

YOUR CHILDREN AND/OR OTHER DEPENDENTS

Names	Relationships	Birth Date	Ages	Sex	Health	Other Information

ILL. 2.1 ■ Sample Fact-Finding Form (continued)

FINANCIAL DATA

Amount

ANNUAL INCOME

Your Current Annual Earnings. . . . .$ _____
    Intend to continue working for how long? _____ If your spouse should die? _____

Spouse's Current Annual Earnings . . . .$ _____
    Intend to continue working for how long? _____ If you should die? _____

Annual Income From Other Sources (investments, trusts, etc.) . . . .$ _____

                    Total Current Annual Income . . . .$ _____

PRESENT GENERAL ASSETS

(List cash, checking and/or savings accounts, U.S. Savings Bonds, other bonds, stocks, mutual funds, residence, other real estate, business interests, vested pension or profit-sharing plans, personal property, other assets)

	Owner*	Approximate Current Liquidation Value	Approximate Current Annual Income
		$	$
Total Present Assets		$	$

*Owner: Y—You; S—Spouse; J—Joint; C—Community Property

PRESENT LIABILITIES

(List mortgage on residence, current bills, installment debts, notes, unpaid taxes, other indebtedness)

	Approximate Balance Owing	Approximate Payments
	$	$
Total Liabilities	$	$

PRESENT LIFE INSURANCE

(On You, Spouse, Children and Dependents, if applicable)

Person Insured	Company	Face Amount	Kind (Include additional benefits)	Issue Age	Policy Loan

ILL. 2.1 ■ Sample Fact-Finding Form (continued)

GOVERNMENT BENEFITS DATA

SOCIAL SECURITY
You: Covered? _____ ; How long? _____ ; % of Max. Earnings? _____ ; Soc. Sec. No. _____
Spouse: Covered? _____ ; How long? _____ ; % of Max. Earnings? _____ ; Soc. Sec. No. _____

MISCELLANEOUS DATA

WILLS
You: Have a will? _____ ; Date _____ ; When last revised? _____ ; Executor _____
Spouse: Have a will? _____ ; Date _____ ; When last revised? _____ ; Executor _____
Have you taken advantage of marital deduction privileges? _____ ; Named a guardian for minors? _____

(Give Name and Address if applicable)

ADVISERS BANKS
Your: Attorney _____
Accountant _____
Bank _____
Spouse's: Attorney _____
Accountant _____
Bank _____

TRUSTS – BEQUESTS – GIFTS – ETC.
Are you or spouse involved in any trusts? _____ ; Any inheritances or bequests? _____ ; Made any gifts? _____
Pertinent data: _____

HEALTH PLANS
You: Disability Income $_____ for _____ years sickness or _____ years accident; Medical Expense _____
Spouse: Disability Income $_____ for _____ years sickness or _____ years accident; Medical Expense _____
Other details _____

PENSION PLANS
You? _____ ; Est. income $_____ at age _____ ; Spouse? _____ ; Est. income $_____ at age _____
Other details _____

OTHER
Is there any other information that might be helpful in evaluating your situation? _____

LOCATION OF IMPORTANT ITEMS
(Safety deposit box and key, bank accounts, marriage license, birth certificates, will, other vital papers, etc.) _____

ILL. 2.1 ■ Sample Fact-Finding Form (continued)

FAMILY FINANCIAL OBJECTIVES

	If You Die	If Spouse Dies		If You Die	If Spouse Dies
FINAL EXPENSE FUND NEEDS			Death taxes:		
Monthly bills, total _____	$ _____	$ _____	Federal _____	$ _____	$ _____
*Installment purchases _____	$ _____	$ _____	State _____	$ _____	$ _____
*Loans _____	$ _____	$ _____	Emergency fund _____	$ _____	$ _____
Doctors, hospital, nurses, funeral _____	$ _____	$ _____	**Bequests _____	$ _____	$ _____
Legal fees, court costs, executor's fee and bond _____	$ _____	$ _____	Other _____	$ _____	$ _____
*Current unpaid taxes _____	$ _____	$ _____	Total Final Expense Fund Needs $ _____		$ _____
*See Page 2			**See Page 3		

HOUSING FUND NEED

	If You Die	If Spouse Dies
Continuation of mortgage payments of ____	$ _____ a month for _____ years	$ _____ a month for _____ years
Or, liquidation of mortgage with _____	Cash of $ _____	Cash of $ _____
Or, rental payments of _____	$ _____ a month for _____ years	$ _____ a month for _____ years
Other arrangement _____		

EDUCATION FUND NEEDS

For (Child):				
If You Die	$	$	$	$
If Spouse Dies	$	$	$	$

MONTHLY INCOME NEEDS

	If You Die	If Spouse Dies		If You Die	If Spouse Dies
Food _____	$ _____	$ _____	Medical and dental care _____	$ _____	$ _____
Clothing (inc. laundry and cleaning)	$ _____	$ _____	Housing payment, if any _____	$ _____	$ _____
Utilities (incl. heat) _____	$ _____	$ _____	Miscellaneous _____	$ _____	$ _____
Home maintenance _____	$ _____	$ _____	Other _____	$ _____	$ _____
Property taxes _____	$ _____	$ _____	Total Immediate Monthly Family Income Needs _____	$ _____	$ _____
Transportation _____	$ _____	$ _____			

TOTAL NEEDS SUMMARY AND PRIORITIES

NEEDS	If YOU Should Die	Order of Priority	If Your SPOUSE Dies	Order of Priority	If You BOTH Live
CASH:					
Final Expense Fund	$ _____	( )	$ _____	( )	
Housing Fund (Lump sum, if any)	$ _____	( )	$ _____	( )	
Education Fund	$ _____	( )	$ _____	( )	
INCOME:					
Children's Dependency Period —					
While more than 1 child under age 18	$ _____	( )	$ _____	( )	
While only 1 child under age 18	$ _____	( )	$ _____	( )	
Spouse's Life Income — to age _____	$ _____	( )			
— For life thereafter	$ _____	( )			
Your Life Income — to age _____			$ _____	( )	
— For life thereafter			$ _____	( )	
RETIREMENT INCOME: At your age _____					$ _____

ADDITIONAL OBJECTIVES (needs and desires): _____

FUNDING   If needed to accomplish the above objectives, how much additional could you set aside? $ _____ per _____

ILL. 2.2 ■ Family Data

FAMILY DATA

Date _____

YOU

Your Name: _____ Birthdate: _____ Health: _____

Home Address: _____ Home Telephone: _____

Occupation: _____ Employer: _____

Business Address: _____ Business Telephone: _____

Do you and/or your spouse own an interest in the business? _____ Details: _____

_____

(If an answer is the same as above or not applicable, write "Same" or "N.A." respectively, in the blank.)

YOUR SPOUSE

Spouse's Name: _____ Marriage Date: _____ Birthdate: _____ Health: _____

Home Address: _____ Home Telephone: _____

Occupation: _____ Employer: _____

Business Address: _____ Business Telephone: _____

Do you and/or your spouse own an interest in the business? _____ Details: _____

_____

YOUR CHILDREN AND/OR OTHER DEPENDENTS

Names	Relationships	Birthdates	Ages	Sex	Health	Other Information

If parents, brothers, sisters, in-laws or others are currently or potentially dependent upon this family's income producers, list their names and ages in addition to the relationship to the prospect, nature and extent of dependency and other pertinent information.

Financial Data

The next section of our sample fact-finding form asks for information about the family's current income and estate (assets and liabilities). Separate spaces are provided for *Annual Income* (Ill. 2.3), *Present General Assets* (Ill. 2.4), *Present Liabilities* (Ill. 2.5) and *Present Life Insurance* (Ill. 2.6).

Certain other assets—government benefits and several miscellaneous items—are covered in other sections.

The *Annual Income* section refers to three possible sources of income: (1) prospect's earnings, (2) spouse's earnings and (3) income from other sources, such as investments. It includes questions about how long each spouse intends to work and how long each spouse will continue working if the other spouse dies. This information is invaluable in determining what income should be available under various circumstances.

Knowledge of all family earnings is essential for establishing reasonable financial objectives and formulating recommendations that fit within the limits of the family's ability to pay. After all, income is the usual source of premium dollars. So don't hesitate to ask about your prospects' incomes. A prospect who is reluctant to discuss income probably is not adequately sold on you and the value of your proposed service and will not respond favorably to your presentation. If this situation exists, either return to the job of selling the basic idea of total needs or go on to another prospect. It's important to bring out and deal with any early doubts the prospect may have. This helps avoid later problems with the sale.

Under *Present General Assets*, list the assets owned by the prospect and spouse separately and jointly or as community property. Also record the prospect's best estimates of the assets' liquidation and income values.

Complete facts about the family's present assets reveal possible sources of premium dollars, future family income and funds to help meet cash requirements in the total needs plan. In a larger estate, an inventory of assets is needed to measure the probable impact of estate settlement costs so that adequate provision can be made for estate liquidity. In such cases you'll want to ascertain whether the prospect intends to leave certain assets intact for the family, e.g., a business.

Personal questions that aren't on the fact-finding form may uncover valuable clues concerning the family's savings and investment habits and preferences. Questions like the following may be especially revealing:

- "Do you have a regular method of saving money?"
- "What are you trying to accomplish with your investment program?"
- "How much do you think you should be saving?"

ILL. 2.3 ■ Annual Income

FINANCIAL DATA

ILL. 2.4 ■ Present General Assets

(List cash, checking and/or savings accounts, U.S. Savings Bonds, other bonds, stocks, mutual funds, residence, other real estate, business interests, vested pension or profit-sharing plans, personal property, other assets)

PRESENT GENERAL ASSETS		Owner*	Approximate Current Liquidation Value	Approximate Current Annual Income
			$	$
	Total Present Assets		$	$

*Owner: Y—You; S—Spouse; J—Joint; C—Community Property

- "Were you satisfied with last year's increase in your net worth?"

A listing of the prospect's liabilities in the next part, *Present Liabilities* (Ill. 2.5), is important for several reasons. Details about the mortgage, are necessary to determine the amount and kind of policy best suited to a mortgage fund. The extent of miscellaneous debts has an important effect on the size of the clean-up fund. Also, knowing the sizes and completion dates of debt payments may be significant when looking for premium dollars.

When inquiring about a home mortgage, discuss whether the family will remain in the home following the death of either spouse. In view of the alternatives, don't assume that a mortgage cancellation fund is necessary just because the home has a mortgage. It is wiser to base your assumption on in-depth questioning.

The final part of the *Financial Data* section deals with present life insurance on the prospect, spouse, children and other dependents. Recording information about the family's present life insurance, especially on the prospect and spouse, always is necessary if you don't review and analyze the policies. Even if you do so, it's still a good idea to give the prospect an opportunity to talk about the family's feelings and

ILL. 2.5 ■ Present Liabilities

(List mortgage on residence, current bills, installment debts, notes, unpaid taxes, other indebtedness)

PRESENT LIABILITIES		Approximate Balance Owing	Approximate Payments
		$	$
	Total Liabilities	$	$

ILL. 2.6 ■ Present Life Insurance

	Person Insured	Company	Face Amount	Kind (Include additional benefits)	Issue Age	Policy Loan
PRESENT LIFE INSURANCE						

(On You, Spouse, Children and Dependents, if applicable)

attitudes about life insurance. The information you receive may be invaluable when selecting policies with the greatest appeal.

You can determine why the prospect bought life insurance by asking questions like these:

- "What do you want your life insurance to do for you?"
- "What purpose did you have in mind when you bought your last policy?"
- "If you were to buy additional life insurance, what would you want it to accomplish?"

A prospect's response may provide helpful tips for your presentation and close. In fact, *why* people buy often is as important as *what* they buy.

Government Benefits Data

The *Government Benefits Data* section of the sample form primarily concerns Social Security benefits to which family members are or may become entitled (see Ill. 2.7). Note that identical questions cover both the prospect and spouse. The reason is that both may be covered, with potential benefits for themselves or their survivors.

The questions provide the basis for determining benefits available from Social Security. *Covered?* requires a "yes" or "no" answer. *How long?* refers to the number of years the prospect has been covered under Social Security. For *% of Max. Earnings?* write in the approximate percentage of maximum credit earnings the prospect has had during his or her working life. Materials in Chapter 3 and the accompanying *Guide to Social Security* booklet will teach you how to calculate this percentage. If you can't readily determine the approximate percentage of maximum earnings for prospects with less than maximum earnings, record earnings for the appropriate number of earning years, so you can determine the exact percentage later.

Incidentally, it's effective to ask each covered spouse to sign a *Social Security Wage Record* request card at this time. These cards usually are provided by life insurance companies or they are available from Social Security offices. Obtaining this information for prospects helps to establish solid client-agent relationships.

ILL. 2.7 ■ Social Security

GOVERNMENT BENEFITS DATA				
SOCIAL	You: Covered? _____;	How long?_____;	% of Max. Earnings?_____;	Soc. Sec. No. _____
SECURITY	Spouse: Covered? _____;	How long?_____;	% of Max. Earnings?_____;	Soc. Sec. No. _____

Miscellaneous Data

The final data-gathering section, is designed to disclose additional information needed to do a competent job of total needs planning and selling (see Ill. 2.8). Responses to the questions about wills indicate whether the prospect is "estate conscious." If there are no wills or existing wills need updating, suggest that the prospect contact an attorney. Record the names of other professional advisers. You may need their aid later.

Whatever you can learn about trusts, inheritances, bequests or gifts is important, particularly as they affect each family member's financial situation. Such information includes the nature of the arrangement, the people and amounts involved, when payable and under what circumstances.

The questions about health insurance are self-explanatory. Even if you do not plan to cover the subject in your presentation, get the information.

Information about pension or profit-sharing plans is also vital. Such plans are often expected to provide a major source of income in prospects' retirement years. By reviewing pamphlets or other material about basic provisions of various plans, you can explain the benefits to prospects and often gain satisfied clients in the process.

Next is the clean-up question—"Is there any other information that . . . ?" Its purpose is to reveal facts previously overlooked or inadequately discussed. Listen carefully to the prospect's answer; you may uncover something especially significant.

Location of Important Items ends the data-gathering exercise. From here, move to the objectives-setting phase of the interview.

■ FAMILY FINANCIAL OBJECTIVES

Setting objectives is important in any kind of life insurance selling. It's a method of helping prospects determine what they really want to accomplish. As mentioned earlier, uncovering personal wants is the basis of motivation. So in total needs selling, setting realistic financial objectives is absolutely necessary. Furthermore, it brings you face-to-face with what may be your most challenging task in total needs selling.

During this phase, first review each of the common family financial needs with the prospect and spouse and explain it in general terms. Next, help the prospect and spouse relate those needs to their own situation. Your challenge is to help prospects plainly see the financial problems their families will face at their death. Unless they have those fundamental needs firmly in mind and accept them as their own, it makes no sense to talk about setting objectives.

ILL. 2.8 ■ Miscellaneous Data

MISCELLANEOUS DATA

WILLS

You: Have a will?_____ ; Date _____ ; When last revised?_____ ; Executor _____
Spouse: Have a will?_____ ; Date _____ ; When last revised?_____ ; Executor _____
Have you taken advantage of marital deduction privileges?_____ ; Named a guardian for minors? _____

_____

(Give Name and Address if applicable)

ADVISERS BANKS

Your: Attorney _____
Accountant _____
Bank _____
Spouse's: Attorney _____
Accountant _____
Bank _____

_____

TRUSTS — BEQUESTS — GIFTS — ETC.

Are you or spouse involved in any trusts?_____ ; Any inheritances or bequests? _____ ; Made any gifts?_____
Pertinent data:_____
_____

HEALTH PLANS

You: Disability Income $_____ for _____ years sickness or _____ years accident; Medical Expense_____
Spouse: Disability Income $_____ for _____ years sickness or _____ years accident; Medical Expense_____
Other details_____

PENSION PLANS

You?_____ ; Est. income $_____ at age _____ ; Spouse? _____ ; Est. income $_____ at age_____
Other details_____

OTHER

Is there any other information that might be helpful in evaluating your situation?_____
_____

LOCATION OF IMPORTANT ITEMS

(Safety deposit box and key, bank accounts, marriage license, birth certificates, will, other vital papers, etc.)_____
_____
_____

The *Family Financial Objectives* portion of the sample form provides a list of the common needs for consideration and discussion and a place to record amounts and priorities. You even can use it as a step-by-step discussion guide.

The first section, *Final Expense Fund Needs* (Ill. 2.9), reflects the amounts of cash required at death to pay the specific expenses listed. The purpose of the first eight items is to clean up all of those obligations, allowing surviving family members to start from that point with a clean financial slate.

The emergency fund is intended to provide money for unforeseen miscellaneous costs and expenses that may arise in the future.

Bequests, too, must be recorded. Additional discussion and notes about the purposes, people involved, etc., may prove invaluable later.

"Other" recognizes that many family situations may reflect special cash needs that are not included under any of the other needs listed, e.g., an "opportunity fund." If such needs exist, discuss and record them.

The prospect must estimate the amounts of many financial objectives. However, you can help by referring to the recorded amounts of liabilities and assets in the *Financial Data* section of the form. The liabilities clearly reflect needed amounts, but assets require some translation. Normally the greater the assets, the larger the legal and administration fees, taxes, probate costs and other expenses. All of these usually must be paid before the surviving family members are paid the balance of the estate.

These are ideas and concepts you should sell to your prospects before attempting to isolate and record specific needs. After prospects understand the purposes and significance of the final expense fund, usually they'll work with you willingly to identify their cash needs and to establish amounts required to cover those needs.

In the *Housing Fund Need* section (Ill. 2.10), the typical cash need at the prospect's death is the amount required to pay off the mortgage, if the family is buying a home. However, don't simply assume that paying off the mortgage is your prospect's or the surviving family's desire. Discuss the alternatives open to surviving family members. For example, the family could use the fund to continue making mortgage payments; perhaps this provides an income tax advantage. The family could wait and sell the home when market conditions are most favorable and then use the proceeds from the sale and/or the housing fund to provide more suitable housing. Or they could retain the home as income-producing rental property. In any event a cash fund can give them an option.

On the other hand, if the family is renting its home now, the need may be for a monthly amount to continue rental payments for a certain number of years. Don't forget that the prospect's attitudes toward a housing fund and other needs may depend upon which spouse's death you're considering.

Most total needs prospects want their children to obtain "a good education," but for how many years, where, how expensive it will be and how it will be paid for are

ILL. 2.9 ■ Final Expense Fund Needs

FAMILY FINANCIAL OBJECTIVES

		If You Die	If Spouse Dies		If You Die	If Spouse Dies
FINAL EXPENSE FUND NEEDS	Monthly bills, total	$	$	Death taxes:		
	*Installment purchases	$	$	Federal	$	$
	*Loans	$	$	State	$	$
	Doctors, hospital, nurses, funeral	$	$	Emergency fund	$	$
				**Bequests	$	$
	Legal fees, court costs, executor's fee and bond	$	$	Other	$	$
	*Current unpaid taxes	$	$	Total Final Expense Fund Needs $		$
	*See Page 2			**See Page 3		

ILL. 2.10 ■ Housing Fund Needs

		If You Die	If Spouse Dies
HOUSING FUND NEED	Continuation of mortgage payments of ____ $_____ a month for _____ years	$_____ a month for _____ years	
	Or, liquidation of mortgage with _____ Cash of $ _____	Cash of $_____	
	Or, rental payments of _____ $_____ a month for _____ years	$_____ a month for _____ years	
	Other arrangement _____ _____	_____	

goals that vary widely among prospects. Discuss these goals with your prospect and record the amount needed in the section *Education Fund Needs*, shown in Ill. 2.11.

It's probably best first to discuss the costs of each child's education because costs can vary according to the child's particular interests or talents, educational ambitions (type of college or specific school, degrees, years) and costs for tuition, books and supplies, room and board and other factors. Then the educational costs for all the children can be totaled. However, that still may not be the final figure because the prospect may not wish to fund the total cost in advance. Many parents feel that educational costs should be partially (or totally) funded from earned income (including the child's income) when the child enters college.

So the next step is to agree on the amount to be funded if the prospect or spouse dies. It's a good idea to consider the probable impact of inflation, especially if the children are young. It also is wise to note separately the amount of funding desired if both prospect and spouse live beyond their children's educational period.

The section, *Monthly Income Needs*, shown as Ill. 2.12, refers to the amounts of income surviving family members will need immediately if either the prospect or spouse dies. Later these total needs will be partially offset by income from various sources, including existing assets, government and other benefit plans, life insurance, the surviving spouse's earnings and other sources. However, the amounts to be established here are the *total* immediate income needs in either eventuality. They should result from in-depth discussions with the prospect and spouse.

Next, all the needs are summarized and prioritized in the next to last section of the form, shown in Ill. 2.13. The three cash item totals—Final Expense Fund, Housing Fund and Education Fund—are obtained easily from immediately preceding parts of the form. The income items, however, require some explanation.

ILL. 2.11 ■ Education Fund Needs

EDUCATION FUND NEEDS	For (Child):				
	If You Die	$	$	$	$
	If Spouse Dies	$	$	$	$

ILL. 2.12 ■ Monthly Income Needs

		If You Die	If Spouse Dies		If You Die	If Spouse Dies
MONTHLY INCOME NEEDS	Food _____	$ _____	$ _____	Medical and dental care _____	$ _____	$ _____
	Clothing (inc. laundry and cleaning)	$ _____	$ _____	Housing payment, if any _____	$ _____	$ _____
	Utilities (incl. heat) _____	$ _____	$ _____	Miscellaneous _____	$ _____	$ _____
	Home maintenance _____	$ _____	$ _____	Other _____	$ _____	$ _____
	Property taxes _____	$ _____	$ _____	Total Immediate Monthly		
	Transportation _____	$ _____	$ _____	Family Income Needs _____	$ _____	$ _____

Children's Dependency Period

This refers to the family's income needs while the children are dependent, usually until the youngest child reaches age 18. The typical total needs prospect wants surviving family members to continue their present standard of living throughout the dependency period. So the amount of income during this period usually should nearly equal the present income level. However, some authorities feel that this level can be reduced safely by amounts previously spent on the deceased's maintenance, the mortgage payments or other expenses that are no longer payable. One study suggested that survivors can continue their present standard of living on 57 percent to 70 percent of previous income. The percentage varies according to family income, ranging from 70 percent of up to $39,000, to 57 percent of more than $53,500. Other authorities make this determination based on the number of surviving family members. Under this method, the income should equal 70 percent of previous income if there are dependent children; if there are no dependent children living at home, the income level should equal 50 percent of previous income.

Sometimes the income currently used to maintain the prospect differs from the amount used to maintain the spouse. In such cases, the dependency period income

ILL. 2.13 ■ Total Needs Summary and Priorities

	NEEDS	If YOU Should Die	Order of Priority	If Your SPOUSE Dies	Order of Priority	If You BOTH Live
TOTAL NEEDS SUMMARY AND PRIORITIES	CASH:					
	Final Expense Fund	$ _____	( )	$ _____	( )	
	Housing Fund (Lump sum, if any)	$ _____	( )	$ _____	( )	
	Education Fund	$ _____	( )	$ _____	( )	
	INCOME:					
	Children's Dependency Period –					
	While more than 1 child under age 18	$ _____	( )	$ _____	( )	
	While only 1 child under age 18	$ _____	( )	$ _____	( )	
	Spouse's Life Income – to age _____	$ _____	( )			
	– For life thereafter	$ _____	( )			
	Your Life Income – to age _____			$ _____	( )	
	– For life thereafter			$ _____	( )	
	RETIREMENT INCOME: At your age _____					$ _____
	ADDITIONAL OBJECTIVES (needs and desires): _____					
FUNDING	If needed to accomplish the above objectives, how much additional could you set aside? $ _____ per _____					

needed at the prospect's death might vary from income needed if the spouse dies. Discuss each situation with the prospect and agree upon an appropriate amount.

Social Security or other government and employee benefit plans frequently are large enough to satisfy somewhat substantial needs. Nevertheless, be sure your prospect understands that, while government benefits may go a long way in meeting the family's needs, it's a good idea to build in some flexibility and growth, particularly in light of the potential effect of inflation on future income.

Spouse's Life Income

The prospect's surviving spouse will need income for life after the children reach adulthood. So this income need extends from the end of the dependency period to the spouse's death. In some families the prospect may wish to provide generously for the surviving spouse, particularly if the spousal relationship is strong. In other cases a prospect may want to provide very modestly, if at all, for the surviving spouse. A common reason is that the spouse currently is working or is capable of earning a good income; so the prospect assumes that the spouse won't require strong income guarantees. Consider these variables when tailoring the total needs plan.

Assuming the prospect wishes to guarantee the spouse's current standard of living, the amount of income established should approximately equal the dependency period income, reduced by income that was needed to maintain the children and by expenses that will end after the children are grown.

Your (the Prospect's) Life Income

The assumption here is that the spouse dies and the prospect is the survivor. Considerations are basically the same as for the spouse's life income, discussed previously. However, the amount of life income may be different because the determining factors—current and future income-earning capacity, etc.—may not be the same.

Retirement Income

The happy eventuality is that both prospect and spouse will live to a ripe old age. Discuss thoroughly their retirement goals, including what they want to do, where they want to live, at what age they anticipate that retirement will begin and how much income will be needed. If the prospect wants to maintain the prior standard of living, the amount of income must stay at approximately the preretirement level. You can adjust it, of course, to reflect payments or expenses that will end and those that the prospect will incur before or after retirement. Examples of reductions might include mortgage payments (if the mortgage is paid off or the home is sold), work-related expenses, certain insurance premiums, etc. Items to add might include rent (if the home is sold), added travel or other recreational expenses, premiums for private replacement of group employee insurance, etc. You may also need to allow for income taxes and sales taxes.

Additional Objectives

This line on our sample form has two purposes. First, it reminds you to ask the prospect for any other objectives that have not been discussed. Second, it provides a convenient place to record those objectives or to make other notes that might prove helpful.

■ HELPFUL RULES OF THUMB

Probably only a few of your prospects have thought seriously about the amount of money that will be required when they die or retire, until you introduce the subject. Cash needs usually are easier to determine than income needs. Because your job includes providing constructive guidance, some simple rules of thumb at least can give you a convenient starting point for discussing income needs.

A general rule is that certain percentages of a prospect's current annual income, as set forth in Ill. 2.14, will be needed during the dependency period and for the surviving spouse's lifetime. This illustration is designed to suggest total income amounts a surviving family may need before deducting income from Social Security, present assets and other sources. It is assumed that the mortgage is paid or a rent fund is established and that children's educations are taken care of separately. The figures reflect percentages mentioned earlier in this unit and are similar to those used by life insurance agents who practice the capital need analysis techniques referred to in the Introduction to this text.

As you review these percentages, keep in mind that they:

1. apply to current total family income—that includes the incomes of both spouses in a two-income family;
2. vary with the total amount of current income—the higher the present income, the lower the percentage because a smaller proportion of income generally is being used now for family support and
3. pertain to gross income figures—income from Social Security and other sources later must be deducted to arrive at the remaining income needs that additional life insurance can satisfy.

An overriding rule of thumb is that regardless of the method used to determine the monthly income objectives for a surviving spouse, be sure to include the *net additional monthly cost* of replacing any housekeeping and child-care services that the deceased spouse provided. This important—and often substantial—addition fre-

ILL. 2.14 ■ Percent of Current Annual Income for Dependency Period and Surviving Spouse's Lifetime

Current Annual Income from All sources	% to Continue During Dependency Period	% to Continue During Spouse's Lifetime
Up to $39,000	70	35
$39,000 to $43,499	66	35
$43,500 to $47,999	63	30
$48,000 to $53,500	60	25
Over $53,500	57	25

Note: If both spouses work, it is suggested that 70 percent of their total gross income should be provided regardless of the income level.

quently is overlooked because it generally is a hidden cost. The *net cost* is the amount by which the additional cost of any outside help *exceeds* the deceased spouse's previous maintenance costs (clothing, food, etc.).

Maintaining Current Standard of Living

By using the above rules of thumb, the prospect can set an income level that allows survivors to continue their accustomed standard of living, as opposed to a minimum standard. Social Security or other government programs, group insurance and other employee benefits furnish a respectable financial base in many cases. Beyond this, current living costs and personal incomes are high and probably will continue to climb. Therefore, today's total needs prospect generally is not impressed with recommended income levels that provide only the bare necessities for survivors or "just enough to get by." This person probably lives in a good neighborhood, has at least two cars and a fine home with the latest conveniences and wants college educations for the children. So to set an income level lower than the family can afford or is accustomed to is a disservice as well as poor business. Nevertheless, the prospect is the final authority. Any rule of thumb should serve only as a guide, not as a hard-and-fast stand.

Setting Need Priorities

Before proceeding to the final section of the fact-finding form review all of the prospect's objectives. Then help the prospect establish priorities for meeting the various financial needs. Begin by asking: "Which of these objectives is most important to you and your family now?" After recording the prospect's first priority, ask similar questions to record the descending order of priorities for the remaining objectives. Note that space is provided for recording priorities on our sample fact-finding form. The prospect's responses are immeasurably important when it's time to develop and present your recommendations.

An Important Decision

Before leaving this part of your fact-finding session, you should decide whether to (1) continue immediately into a *one-interview* selling effort or (2) arrange an appointment to return later with your analyses and recommendations. By using the one-interview method, you either make the sale quickly or—if the prospect absolutely isn't going to buy—avoid time wasted in lengthy preparation. Also, by striking while the iron is hot, you don't have to reestablish the prospect's needs before making your presentation and closing attempts.

Alternatively, you might prefer the *two-interview* method in all but the simplest cases for several reasons. First, the additional time permits you to analyze the situation thoroughly and prepare your presentation, enhancing the chance of making the sale. Second, making the prospect feel that you are evaluating the facts carefully and unhurriedly may give you a psychological advantage. Third, the prospect doesn't have a direct view of the sometimes complicated process of deciding what to recommend and how to present those recommendations.

Because both methods have advantages and disadvantages, base your choice on the particular circumstances in each case. For example, if the "engineering" can be done quickly and efficiently in the prospect's presence, you may decide to use the one-interview method. Conversely, if the complexities of the case demand in-depth analysis, calculations and planning, the two-interview method probably is better.

In any event, if the prospect's insurability is questionable, it's usually best to break after the fact-finding phase and seek an answer before continuing. Your recommendations then will be based on that answer.

■ GETTING A COMMITMENT

The final step in fact-finding is to obtain a definite commitment from the prospect. At this point, you want some sort of positive reaction to confirm that the prospect is sincerely interested in solving the financial problems that you both have considered. If you don't get a reasonable commitment, generally you shouldn't proceed with the case because the prospect isn't sufficiently disturbed about the family's financial situation. Consider bowing out graciously or attempting to close a smaller package sale. Try again if you still feel the prospect eventually might become a client.

Types of Commitments

Generally, there are four types of commitments. According to their relative value they are

1. a definite premium commitment;
2. a definite appointment for a medical exam;
3. a definite appointment for the next interview and
4. picking up the prospect's policies.

Premium Commitment

A premium commitment is at the top of the list for three reasons. First, it practically assures that a sale will be made, assuming you conduct a reasonably effective presentation. Second, it enables you to recommend the policy best suited to the prospect's individual circumstances. Third, it is appropriate in *both* one-interview and two-interview selling, whereas the other commitments apply only in two-interview selling. Securing a premium commitment mainly entails a straightforward request, like the one in the last section of the sample fact finder: "If needed to accomplish the above objectives, how much additional could you set aside? $ _____ per _____?"

Of course, you don't want a commitment that doesn't fit the prospect's income because this increases the chance of a lapsed policy. Sometimes, questions like the following will help the prospect to arrive at a reasonable figure:

- "If you put your mind to it, do you think you might be able to set aside more than this amount?"
- "Is there a chance this amount could put too great a strain on your budget right now?"

Appointment for a Medical Exam

Arranging a medical exam is especially worthwhile if there is any reason to question the prospect's insurability. You can treat the examination as a routine part of the fact-finding process. It almost requires the two-interview method, because a rating or rejection can affect recommendations, ranging from election of dividend additions to immediate conversion of any reducing term insurance. Many agents routinely set up a medical exam in every case because it puts them in a position to order a policy for presentation during the selling interview.

Appointment for the Next Interview

When using the two-interview method, obtain a definite appointment for the next interview. Otherwise you're neglecting basic rules of self organization and time control.

Picking Up the Policies

This applies only if you plan a two-interview sale. While it's true that this step commits a prospect to another interview for all practical purposes, you might want to think twice before deciding to take it.

The policies of several prospects can pile up in your office, increasing the danger of misplacing or losing them. More importantly, if the policies are picked up, both you and the prospect are inclined to feel that a detailed audit is in order. Usually an audit at this point is premature. Until you complete the sales presentation and the prospect has a chance to act on your suggestions, a complete policy analysis is often just busywork.

■ FACT-FINDING WRAP-UP

Skillful fact-finding alone won't guarantee success. However, the ability to meet the objectives we've discussed consistently will contribute substantially to your growth and development.

The selling phase will present no great problems if you've conducted a prior fact-finding discussion along the lines described here. With a clear understanding of the prospect's objectives and a definite premium commitment, you can develop an attractive, realistic and salable recommendation. Equally important, you'll have a reservoir of background information with which to establish a long-standing client-counselor relationship.

As pointed out earlier, many established agents say that fact-finding is the most critical phase in developing quality sales. To help prospects motivate themselves, you need a clear understanding of their personal and financial affairs and objectives. This phase provides the insight and knowledge that enable you to convert prospects to clients who call you "my life insurance agent."

■ CHAPTER 2 QUESTIONS FOR REVIEW

1. If a prospect is reluctant to discuss income during the fact-finding phase, it likely means that the:

   a. prospect's income is so high that he or she does not want to disclose it.
   b. prospect's income is so low that he or she does not want to admit it.
   c. prospect feels that questions about income are not valid.
   d. prospect does not completely trust the life insurance agent and hasn't bought into the program being offered.

2. When discussing the housing fund need, the life insurance agent should:

   a. assume that the mortgage must be paid off.
   b. discuss possible alternatives for the survivors.
   c. point out that the family will have to move to cheaper housing if the breadwinner dies.
   d. stress the advantages that home ownership has over renting.

3. The net additional monthly cost of housekeeping and child-care services can be figured by:

   a. subtracting the deceased spouse's salary from the current household income.
   b. subtracting the deceased spouse's maintenance costs from the total household maintenance costs.
   c. determining if the additional cost of household and child-care help exceeds the deceased spouse's maintenance costs.
   d. adding child-care and household costs to the deceased spouse's maintenance costs.

4. The spouse's life income need extends:

   a. from the breadwinner's death until the children leave home.
   b. from the end of the child dependency period until the spouse's death.
   c. from the breadwinner's death until the spouse's death.
   d. until the children are all self-supporting.

5. The *Annual Income* section of the fact-finding form lists income from:

   a. the prospect's earnings.
   b. sources such as investments.
   c. the spouse's earnings.
   d. All of the above

3

Social Security Benefits

T his chapter shows you how to estimate and explain Social Security benefits to your clients. Special terms are defined and case illustrations are included to help you use the accompanying *Guide to Social Security*. This knowledge will enable you to show clients how life insurance can fill the income gap that Social Security does not satisfy.

■ ■ ■ ■ ■

The federal government established the Social Security system in 1935. Since then, Social Security has become a tremendous economic and social force, covering nearly every income earner. It is a very important aspect of financial planning.

■ RELATION TO LIFE INSURANCE

A quick look at the scope and purpose of Social Security reveals that this system and life insurance are directly related. In effect, Social Security is a nationwide, "group protective" plan that is financed by taxes on income. Its purpose is to help reduce the financial needs and hardships that arise when a worker dies prematurely, becomes disabled or grows too old to work.

Your main reason for studying Social Security, however, is that while it does provide valuable coverage for many of your prospects and policyowners, it does not do the whole job. Often it falls short of protecting future needs and simply gives a base upon which to build with personal life insurance.

Few people clearly understand the potential benefits Social Security offers, even though these benefits may represent thousands of dollars in the event of death, disability or retirement. You can offer a valuable service and build goodwill by providing this information. However, you must know how to estimate, apply and explain these benefits.[*]

Social Security and life insurance have the same objectives, but Social Security generally is unable to satisfy these objectives completely. It is obvious that Social Security benefits and life insurance should be closely coordinated.

You must have a working knowledge of Social Security, however, before learning more about total needs selling concepts. Without that knowledge, you will be unable to tell policyowners and prospects what their Social Security benefits will and won't do for them and their families.

You must be able to translate the complex language of the law into simple, everyday terms that the average person can understand. The Social Security Act covers hundreds of pages filled with all kinds of "whereof" and "whereas" and special terms that only an expert can interpret. It's no wonder that many people are confused about what the program will do for them.

That's where you come in, and that's the reason for this chapter: to give you the basic facts about Social Security in simple language. Then you can make this information part of your sales story.

We have found from experience that most people are interested primarily in the answers to four questions:

1. Who gets the Social Security benefits?
2. When will they get them?
3. How much will they amount to?
4. Is there a chance of losing them?

You will find the answers to these vitally important questions in the pages that follow, together with the *Guide to Social Security* accompanying this text. This chapter contains general information about the Social Security law, and the *Guide* provides details on benefit amounts.

Your Opportunity

Social Security is a great door-opener. When people have money coming—real money, amounting to many thousands of dollars—they certainly want to hear about it. So a practical knowledge of Social Security will give you an entry to many prospects who might otherwise be difficult to approach. Naturally, the more people you see, the greater your opportunity for making sales and performing services that will lead to future sales.

Even more important, your knowledge of Social Security will enable you to show prospects where their potential benefits fall short of providing adequately for family

---

[*] The Social Security figures and tables presented in this and subsequent chapters are examples for teaching purposes only. For the most current information, see the latest edition of the *Guide to Social Security*.

and old-age needs. Of course, you will explain that life insurance is the ideal medium for completing their financial plans. Here again, this chapter should be of appreciable help to you because it points out the tragic losses of Social Security benefits that may result if your prospects fail to take care of the gaps and weak spots in their programs.

■ SOCIAL SECURITY AND THE LIFE INSURANCE AGENT

The Social Security program today brings the need for income for the future to the attention of millions of people who might otherwise neglect the problem.

Promoting Income Consciousness

Social Security has made the nation income conscious. This simplifies your work as a life insurance agent in that you can devote less time to stressing the problem of income. You can give more of your time to helping your prospects set up plans to provide adequate incomes for themselves and their dependents.

Furthermore, without Social Security as a foundation for income programs, millions would find the task of making reasonably adequate income provisions virtually impossible. But with basic Social Security income, the task becomes a lot easier. In fact, helping to create supplementary income on top of Social Security income increases the chance that full Social Security benefits will be paid. This obviously opens the way for added services on your part.

Every paycheck with a Social Security deduction says to the income earner, "You must make provisions for the future. The time will come when there will be no more paychecks for you or for your family!" Thus, as far as your work is concerned, the Social Security Act serves to make people conscious of the need to provide for the days when there no longer will be paychecks.

■ THE SOCIAL SECURITY PROGRAM

The total Social Security program covers not only dependency, old age and disability incomes, but also many auxiliary public assistance fields—including "Medicare," the medical care plan for the elderly.

In your work, however, you are primarily concerned with Title II of the Social Security Act—Old-Age, Survivor's and Disability Insurance (OASDI). A fundamental knowledge of the major provisions is important because they:

1. provide an attention-getting approach for interviews;
2. must be considered in all financial planning;
3. must be coordinated with life insurance so Social Security benefits will not be lost and life insurance will provide the greatest overall value;
4. indicate areas in a financial plan that are inadequately covered by Social Security and
5. help you build future prospects for advanced underwriting sales (business insurance, estate planning) because of your initial total needs selling work with clients during which you explain Social Security.

■ SOCIAL SECURITY COVERAGES

Who is covered by Social Security? Who is excluded? The following quick-reference outline will help you determine whether your prospects are eligible. Then you can prepare the most appropriate and effective presentation for each situation.

Compulsory Coverage

Almost every employee or self-employed person is covered under Social Security. In most cases coverage is compulsory. This includes all federal government employees hired after December 31, 1983, as well as employees hired before that date not participating in the Civil Service Retirement program. Also, after December 31, 1983, coverage is mandatory for all members of Congress, the president and vice president of the United States, all sitting federal judges, all executive-level and senior executive service political appointees and all employees of nonprofit organizations.

Voluntary Coverage

For certain groups, coverage normally is voluntary:

1. Members of the clergy may be excluded if they applied for exclusion prior to 1970 or within two years after becoming clergy members. However, ministers, Christian Science practitioners and members of religious sects opposed to public or private insurance generally have compulsory coverage for self-employed income after 1967.
2. State and local government employees are covered if the state elects to enter into an agreement with the federal government. Currently, approximately 80 percent of such employees are covered by Social Security. After July 1, 1991, all state and local government units that provide no pension plan are covered by Social Security.

Groups Excluded from Coverage

The following groups generally are excluded from coverage under Social Security:

1. All federal government employees hired before January 1, 1984, and covered by a federally established retirement system, including Civil Service, are excluded. Military personnel have been covered by Social Security since 1957.
2. Employees under the Railroad Retirement system are excluded.

■ USING THE *GUIDE TO SOCIAL SECURITY*

As mentioned earlier, some features of Social Security are subject to frequent change. For a synopsis of the latest amendments see the front section of the *Guide to Social Security*, which is included with this text.

Next, read each section of the *Guide*. Sections one, two and three of the *Guide* discuss:

1. persons covered;
2. benefits provided and who receives them and

3. what it costs (who pays).

A detailed discussion of these three topics follows later. In section two you'll find a chart showing who most often receives benefits if a worker retires, becomes disabled or dies. Included in section three is a table entitled "Schedule of Social Security Taxes" that shows Social Security tax rates, the maximum amount of earnings taxed and the maximum employee tax. The income tax treatment of Social Security benefits also is covered in section three. Together, these three sections will give you general background knowledge.

Detailed discussions of retirement, disability and death benefits, along with easy-reference tables, are contained in *Guide* sections four through seven. Steps describing how to figure benefits also are included, along with examples for typical situations. The retirement section also tells how benefits may be reduced or lost if the recipient works and gives the actual reduction amounts. This information is particularly helpful when you talk to a prospect about working after retirement or about whether a surviving spouse should work if a covered worker dies.

A clear understanding of Social Security requires familiarity with its special language and methods of determining benefit amounts. Use the *Guide* to make sure you understand the meanings and uses of these terms:

- *Quarter of coverage.* In general, under Social Security rules, you receive one quarter of coverage for a specified amount of wages or salary paid to you in covered employment during a specified period of time. For example, before 1978, you received one quarter of coverage for at least $50 in earnings in a calendar quarter. In 1978, this was changed and now you receive one quarter of coverage for each specified amount of annual earnings. The amount of annual earnings is subject to yearly escalation, e.g., you received one quarter of coverage for each $390 of annual earnings in 1984; one for each $410 of annual earnings in 1985 and one for each $570 of annual earnings in 1992. Quarters of coverage are used to determine your "insured status" under Social Security—fully insured or currently insured.
- *Fully insured.* To be fully insured and qualify for benefits, you must have a required number of quarters of coverage under Social Security.
- *Currently insured.* If you are currently insured, you do not have the required number of quarters of coverage for fully insured status. However, if you are currently insured, you are eligible for some—not all—Social Security benefits.
- *Primary insurance amount* (PIA). Your PIA is the amount you would receive if you retired at your normal retirement age. If you retire earlier, the amount you receive will be less than your PIA. Survivor benefits are based on your PIA at the time you die. If you become disabled, your disability benefit is equal to your PIA at the time disability occurred. To find out your PIA, you must know your earnings history because your PIA is based on your average indexed monthly earnings (AIME).
- *Average indexed monthly earnings* (AIME). Your AIME is calculated by formula, using your earnings history and an index factor that makes past earnings comparable to the level of earnings today. After you have calculated your AIME, you can use the convenient "Table of Monthly Social Se-

curity Benefits" in the *Guide* to determine your PIA and the approximate amount of benefits that you can receive.

Learn how to calculate the AIME and PIA amounts by formula and, more importantly, become adept at estimating benefits quickly by using the easy-reference tables in the *Guide*.

Other Information

Section seven of the *Guide* discusses survivor benefits. Note that there is a lump-sum death benefit of $255 payable to a surviving spouse or to children who are eligible for monthly benefits based on the deceased's earnings record. Qualifications for survivor benefits are an important issue for survivors who receive monthly benefits or the lump-sum death payment. The *Guide* explains this issue and provides examples of family benefits based on the PIA.

Section eight of the *Guide* contains a detailed discussion of the qualification requirements and benefits for Parts A and B of Medicare. Section nine describes in chronological order what steps your prospects or clients should take and when to take them to assure they receive the proper amount of Social Security benefits at time of eligibility. Clients must file for benefits to receive them; so it's important that you relate the proper filing procedures to them. Inserted in the back of the *Guide* is a "Request For Statement of Earnings" card that you can mail to the Social Security Administration to receive the amount of a prospect's credited earnings and quarters of coverage. Obtain extra cards from the Social Security Administration or your company

"Social Security Rules," found in section ten of the *Guide*, contains the general rules used to determine the number of quarters of coverage needed for fully insured status and the number of years of earnings needed to figure the average indexed monthly earnings (AIME) for retirement, disability and death benefits. For workers who retire early and their spouses, as well as surviving spouses who elect to receive benefits prior to normal retirement age, this section contains the factors used to determine the normal retirement age benefit reduction.

■ WHO GETS BENEFITS?

Exactly who will receive Social Security benefits depends on the individual worker's (anyone employed in work covered by Social Security) "insured status." Qualifications are different for different kinds of benefits. Certain persons will be entitled to benefits only if the worker has attained a fully insured status. Others may receive benefits even if the worker is only currently insured.

Fully Insured Benefits

When workers are fully insured the following people can count on Social Security payments:

- *The worker, at retirement.* Full monthly lifetime benefits start at "100% (or Normal) Retirement Age" for a fully insured worker. The "100% (or Normal) Retirement Age" varies with the year of a worker's, spouse's or widow(er)'s birth. For individuals born before 1938, it is age 65; for those born from 1938 to 1943, it gradually rises to age 66; for those born from 1943 to 1955, it is age 66; for those born from 1955 to 1960, it gradually rises to age 67; then for those born after 1960, it remains age 67.

The worker may retire somewhat earlier with a reduced lifetime benefit. The longer retirement is deferred, the larger the lifetime benefit, until the worker reaches the full amount at the "100% (or Normal) Retirement Age." Note that this amount is the "100% Retirement Age" primary insurance amount (PIA)—the base for determining the "100% Retirement Age" retirement benefits.

- *The worker, if disabled.* Should the fully insured worker become seriously disabled, he or she may be entitled to an income before retirement called "disability income." Note that this amount is the current year's disability primary insurance amount (PIA)—the base for determining current disability benefits.

Disability means that you are so severely disabled, mentally or physically, that you cannot perform any substantial gainful work. The disability must be expected to last at least twelve months or to result in earlier death.

- *The worker's spouse, when the worker retires or becomes disabled.* The spouse of an individual who is receiving old-age or disability benefits also is entitled to monthly benefits at his or her "100% (or Normal) Retirement Age" if married to that individual for at least one year or if they are the natural or adoptive parents of a child. The spouse may take reduced benefits as early as age 62.

Should the spouse elect to take a reduced income before his or her "100% (or Normal) Retirement Age," it will continue at that reduced level so long as the spouse and worker live. Should the worker die first, the spouse's benefit will increase to the higher widow(er)'s benefit.

But let's get back to the benefit for the spouse of the retired or disabled worker who has *not* died. Regardless of age, an eligible spouse will get a spouse's benefit if caring for a child of the worker, provided the child is under age 16 (or is disabled) and thus entitled to a benefit. This income to the spouse will stop when the child reaches age 16 (unless disabled)—or earlier, if the child becomes ineligible for a benefit. A child's benefit, however, continues until the eligible child reaches age 18. Of course, the spouse will be entitled to a benefit again at (1) age 62 or over, (2) age 60 or over if a surviving spouse at that time or (3) age 50 to 60 if disabled.

- *The worker's children, when the worker retires or becomes disabled.* If the worker is being paid a retirement or disability benefit, each dependent, unmarried child also is entitled to a monthly benefit until age 18. By definition, a child may be a natural or adopted child, a stepchild or, in some cases, a grandchild of a person receiving benefits.

The child's benefit can continue beyond age 18 if the child is totally and permanently disabled. In this event, the spouse's benefit will not stop at the child's age 16, but will continue until the child recovers and is able to earn a living, or until he or she marries someone who is not receiving a Social Security dependency benefit also.

- *The worker's widow or widower.* The widow or widower of a deceased fully insured worker is entitled to a full monthly benefit at his or her "100% (or Normal) Retirement Age" or has the option of taking a reduced benefit as early as age 60—age 50, if disabled. Generally, the survivor must have been married to the deceased worker for at least nine months or must be the natural or adoptive parent of the worker's child. The benefits are not payable if the survivor has remarried before becoming eligible but may be paid in the event of remarriage after becoming eligible. Note that the "100% (or Normal) Retirement Age" amount is the same as the current year's death primary insurance amount (PIA)—the base for determining death or survivor benefits.

- *The deceased worker's children.* The unmarried children of a deceased fully insured (or currently insured) worker, whether or not there is an eligible surviving spouse, are entitled to monthly benefits to age 18 or beyond if disabled.

- *The worker's widow(er) and children.* While the surviving spouse of a deceased fully insured (or currently insured) individual is caring for one or more children of the deceased who are under age 16 and are unmarried (or disabled), the surviving spouse is entitled to a monthly benefit regardless of the spouse's age. (Continuation of a child's benefit to the child's age 18 does not entitle the spouse to benefits beyond the child's age 16.) This provision also applies to a divorced former spouse of the deceased who is eligible for benefits on the deceased's account. Normally, the benefits terminate when the surviving spouse or former spouse remarries. Keep in mind that the surviving spouse's benefits are in addition to the benefits payable to the children. Although the surviving spouse's benefits cease when the youngest child reaches age 16 (unless disabled), the surviving spouse (or eligible divorced former spouse) of a fully insured worker may again receive a surviving spouse's benefit as early as age 60.

Currently Insured Benefits

Even if the worker is only currently insured (has six quarters of coverage that were earned during the last 13 calendar quarters ending with the quarter in which the worker died), Social Security benefits still will be payable as follows:

- *The worker's surviving spouse and children.* We've already indicated that, so long as a deceased fully insured or currently insured worker's children are under age 16 (or are disabled) and unmarried, the children and an eligible surviving spouse (or eligible divorced former spouse) will receive benefits. Benefits to the children continue to age 18, or beyond if they are disabled.

But when a surviving spouse (or divorced former spouse) of a currently insured worker is no longer entitled to a benefit by having in his or her care a child of the deceased worker under age 16 (or who is disabled), the surviving spouse's (or divorced former spouse's) Social Security income ends permanently. Under the currently insured eligibility provisions, he or she will *not* be eligible for a survivor's old-age benefit in later years.

Lump-Sum Death Benefit

A lump-sum death benefit of $255 is payable to an eligible surviving spouse (or if no eligible spouse, to an eligible surviving child) at the death of a currently or fully insured worker. No one else may be eligible for or receive this benefit.

■ HOW MUCH ARE THE BENEFITS?

Technically, the amount payable to a retired or disabled worker—or to each eligible member of a retired, disabled or deceased worker's family—depends on the size of the worker's primary insurance amount (PIA). As noted earlier, the worker's PIA is determined by complex formulas set out in the Social Security law and applies to the worker's credited earnings during the prescribed earning periods. In general, the higher the credited earnings, the greater the PIA and the larger the benefits, up to certain maximum limits.

As a practical measure, however, you may approximate an individual's percentage of maximum credited earnings and then read the benefits directly from the benefit table in the *Guide to Social Security*. These figures are not exact and never should be so represented or used with respect to actual claims. Only the Social Security Administration can provide exact amounts and then only at the time of the claim. But these benefit figures are close enough for your purposes in total needs selling.

Locate the "Table of Monthly Social Security Benefits" in the *Guide* and follow the steps outlined there for estimating the approximate benefits applicable to a worker and/or members of the worker's family. Review these steps occasionally to keep the procedure well in mind. You may be called on to use it at unexpected times.

Limit on Total Payments

The total benefits payable to a worker's family cannot be greater than the appropriate amount shown in the "Table of Monthly Social Security Benefits" in the *Guide*. If the sum of all eligible persons' benefits (as shown in the table) exceeds the appropriate maximum amount, each person's monthly benefit—other than a retirement or disability monthly benefit—is reduced proportionately so that the reduced total equals that appropriate maximum. A retired or disabled worker's benefit is not reduced and a divorced former spouse's benefit is not considered to be part of the total family benefits.

So in using the benefit table, be careful not to count on any family member receiving the amount shown unless total benefits to all eligible persons fall within the appropriate maximum listed. If total benefits exceed the maximum, the mathematical procedure for reducing each benefit is a little complicated. For the exact formula refer to the *Guide*.

■ WHO PAYS FOR SOCIAL SECURITY BENEFITS?

Social Security is supported by a special tax on personal earnings. The rate of tax depends on whether workers are salaried or are self-employed.

If a worker is salaried, his or her employer deducts the tax from the worker's paychecks until the tax has been paid on the maximum amount taxable for the year. The employer pays an amount of tax equal to the employer's contribution.

The self-employed person, prior to 1984, had a somewhat higher Social Security tax rate than the salaried person's rate. But as of 1984, the amount of tax the self-employed individual pays is equal to the combined amount paid by employee and employer.

The self-employed tax rate is applied to "net income," which means personal earnings less expenses involved in realizing such earnings. But in no case will the self-employed individual pay taxes on more than the current Maximum Wage Base.

■ CAN SOCIAL SECURITY BENEFITS BE LOST?

Monthly benefits can be lost, wholly or in part. A beneficiary can work and earn a limited amount without sacrificing benefits. Beyond this earnings ceiling, Social Security payments begin to erode. So if either a retiree or a surviving spouse is forced to work to supplement Social Security benefits, these benefits can evaporate alarmingly and losses over the years could run into many thousands of dollars. If a retired beneficiary loses benefits, the payments to eligible dependents also are subject to loss. In the case of a surviving spouse who works, however, the children's benefits will not be reduced. In fact, if they had been reduced to satisfy the maximum family benefit, the children's benefits would be increased as a result of the surviving spouse's benefit loss.

Consider, too, the expenses of working that would be added to Social Security benefit losses: extra clothes needed, lunches, transportation, possibly a day-care nursery for a young child, increased income and continuing Social Security taxes. You can see that the added income from working might be reduced to peanuts.

Your prospects want to be sure of getting all the benefits due them. Point out to them how tragic it will be if Social Security benefits are lost. When you talk to prospects about their retirement needs, you might ask, "Isn't it vitally important that you plan to supplement your Social Security with an income that does not carry the penalty of lost benefits?"

Or when interviewing a family breadwinner and discussing the family situation if the surviving spouse had to work to make ends meet, say: "The loss of benefits and all of the expenses of working might add up to defeat and hopelessness, with a parent's love and care traded for what turns out to be a mere pittance. And all of this can be avoided by additional income from life insurance."

■ HOLES IN THE SOCIAL SECURITY PROGRAM

Like a life insurance program, Social Security is simply a series of benefit "packages." To a limited extent, it provides for four needs.

1. Cash for last expenses
2. Dependency period income
3. Surviving spouse's old-age income

4. Retirement income

When we set down the total number of needs and the total dollar needs that must be satisfied before people achieve financial security for themselves and their families, we see large, gaping holes that Social Security does not fill adequately or is not intended to fill at all. These are the holes into which life insurance dollars can and should be poured.

Cash for Last Expenses

Social Security provides only a few dollars of lump-sum death benefits ($255), no matter how high a person's wages. With final expenses as great as they are today, this small benefit is of little help. Add together the probable expenses of last illness and burial, unpaid debts, taxes, probate costs, lawyers' fees, etc., and it's obvious that life insurance proceeds of $5,000 to $8,000, and likely much more, are a must.

A Surviving Spouse's Mortgage Burden

While workers are living, their home is one of their finest assets, even though it carries a mortgage. But when they die, the home immediately is converted into a burden of debt on the shoulders of the surviving spouse.

Social Security makes no provision for paying off the indebtedness on the home. This debt *must* be paid to avoid serious losses: the loss of the home or loss of a parent's care for the children if the surviving spouse has to earn extra income to pay the mortgage—income which may, in turn, cause the loss of many thousands of dollars in Social Security benefits.

A mortgage policy wipes out the danger of these losses. It pays off the mortgage principal, eliminates the added burden of future interest, saves a fortune in benefits, gives the surviving spouse a fighting chance to pay the bills and keeps the family at home during the years in which the children's characters and habits are formed.

There is no doubt about it, this large hole should be pointed out to your prospects and filled in with one of the appropriate policies you can make available so easily.

Emergency Needs

Social Security sets up no extra funds for family emergencies that jolt the surviving spouse's often limited budget: a furnace breakdown, termites in the basement, a graduation suit or dress or an orthodontist's bill for a child.

These are the same kinds of special needs that crop up now to disrupt your prospects' budgets. Again, Social Security provides no cash or loan values to fall back on.

Life insurance is essential to fill the need for emergency reserves, whether your prospect is alive or dead.

Education Fund Need

The costs of college educations are unbelievably high, currently ranging up to about $20,000 for four years in state universities and $60,000 in private institutions. And they increase every year. The U.S. Department of Education recently reported that by the year 2006, the cost of four years at a public university will be $60,000. The cost of an education at a private university will be $200,000.

Yet, the costs of skipping college are even higher. Studies show that college graduates currently enjoy about $385,000 more lifetime earnings, on the average, than do their noncollege peers—to say nothing of the priceless intangible values gained from the college experience. Parents want to assure their children the benefits of college educations and the ability to compete with their college-trained peers.

With cash value life insurance, they can be sure that the needed college funds will be there.

The Blackout Period

Social Security is not designed to take care of a family's total needs for income. Even maximum benefits won't cover all of the essentials in the average home. But although income from Social Security is far from sufficient, it does provide a considerable boost in a person's hopes of achieving a respectable level of family security.

Your responsibility—and opportunity as a life insurance agent—is to help your prospects elevate their sights and to climb to higher levels of security with additional steps of life insurance income.

We have seen that a surviving spouse and children get a Social Security income while the first child is below age 18 and all succeeding children are below age 16. Then, unless a child is disabled, the surviving spouse's benefit is unavailable until the surviving spouse reaches retirement age. Only the child's benefit continues until the child is age 18. Because few parents are past their forties or early fifties by the time the youngest child reaches age 18 this leaves the surviving spouse without Social Security income for a long, difficult period of years called the "blackout period." See Ill. 3.1 for an example of the blackout period.

When both parents work, their combined income provides a higher standard of living than the family would enjoy otherwise. Should one of the parents die, the job of maintaining that living standard is tough while the children are growing up. Social Security affords some help. But the job becomes much tougher after the children are grown. There is no help from Social Security during the blackout period.

In a case in which a nonworking spouse say, a nonworking mother, is the survivor, maintaining a reasonable standard of living during the Social Security blackout period is very difficult. If she has too little income or no income at all, what can she do? Can she find satisfactory work? Even if she worked in previous years, she probably lost contact with the business world during the time she cared for the children. If she can find a job that pays a decent wage, can she hold it against the competition of younger, more skillful people? Will the boss let her go at the first sign of a business slowdown?

If she can't work, how will she feel about turning to the children for a home and care? No doubt she would hate to become a burden on them, right at the time they are trying to get their own homes started or establish themselves in business. Or if she refuses to burden the children, what then? Charity?

ILL. 3.1 ■ The Blackout Period

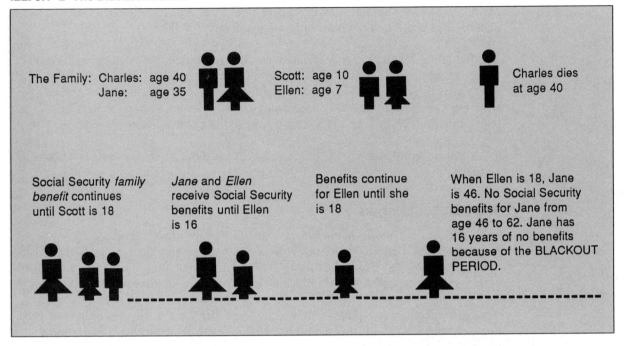

The Family: Charles: age 40   Scott: age 10   Charles dies
Jane: age 35   Ellen: age 7   at age 40

Social Security *family benefit* continues until Scott is 18

Jane and *Ellen* receive Social Security benefits until Ellen is 16

Benefits continue for Ellen until she is 18

When Ellen is 18, Jane is 46. No Social Security benefits for Jane from age 46 to 62. Jane has 16 years of no benefits because of the BLACKOUT PERIOD.

These are the kinds of questions you must bring to your prospects' attention. It's far better that they face them now, rather than force their surviving spouses to face them during the blackout period. And if a surviving spouse's working may be impossible, if living with the children is highly undesirable, if charity is unthinkable—what is the solution to the blackout period problem? Insurance, of course! The required amount of insurance to pay a livable income during the time the surviving spouse receives no Social Security can be specifically arranged.

The One-Child Hazard

When you see a family with only one young child, you also see a great potential loss of Social Security benefits.

The law provides that a surviving spouse is eligible to receive benefits just so long as he or she is caring for a child who is under age 16 or disabled, and thus entitled to benefits. Moreover, the child's benefit continues to the child's age 18. If the child should die, both the child's benefit and the surviving spouse's benefit cease. See Ill. 3.2 for an example of the one-child hazard.

We are all familiar with the income losses that result from the death of a breadwinner. But, aside from the heartache, consider the financial blow facing the surviving spouse at the child's death.

This is another big need to be filled. And the material for filling it is obvious—a policy on the child's life in an amount equal to the total potential loss of benefits—or at least the portion of those benefits that represents the surviving spouse's share.

ILL. 3.2 ■ The One-Child Hazard

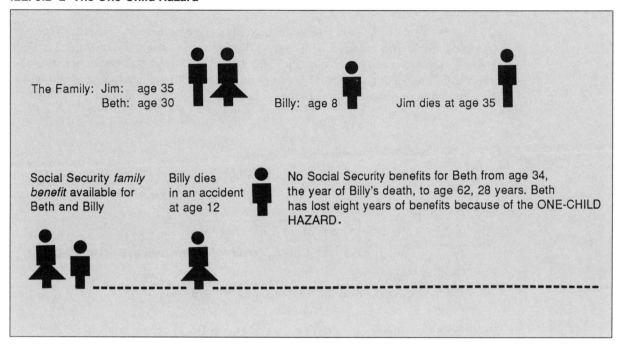

The Family: Jim: age 35
             Beth: age 30

Billy: age 8

Jim dies at age 35

Social Security *family* *benefit* available for Beth and Billy

Billy dies in an accident at age 12

No Social Security benefits for Beth from age 34, the year of Billy's death, to age 62, 28 years. Beth has lost eight years of benefits because of the ONE-CHILD HAZARD.

The Surviving Spouse's Old-Age Income

With income each month from Social Security, a surviving spouse is not completely destitute. But he or she never will have a dignified independence with that income alone.

Everything that has been said about the blackout period can be repeated here, but with greater emphasis. The problem can be especially acute in the case of a non-working surviving spouse. When a person is elderly, finding and holding a job is very difficult.

There's an answer to the problem: more income from insurance to supplement the surviving spouse's modest Social Security benefit.

Roughly speaking, it takes about $10,000 of insurance on a spouse's life to provide an extra $50 a month for the other spouse to supplement Social Security. For $100 a month in addition to Social Security, it would require about $20,000 of insurance.

Retirement

Throughout life, most people strive for higher incomes and a better standard of living. When they decide it's time to "take it easy" and live a little, they want enough money to afford the good things of life. A Social Security income will provide a husband and wife with some of life's necessities but none of the extras many people desire for their retirement years.

Without additional income, the couple must either depend upon income from other sources or continue working, which, as noted, could cause them to forfeit all or a portion of their Social Security benefits. Life insurance is needed as a guaranteed source of income.

■ CASE ILLUSTRATIONS

Let's apply some of the facts you've learned about Social Security benefits. Three examples will be presented for you to work through. Also study the examples in the *Guide to Social Security* carefully. Please note that we are working with approximations only. When using the Social Security tables, refer to the age brackets and income columns that come closest to the facts of each situation presented.

Survivor Benefits—Example I

Here are some facts about Joe Smith and his family:

- Joe is age 50 when he dies.
- At his death he was earning $42,000 annually.
- Joe's dependents include Kathy, his surviving spouse, age 46 and Mary, his daughter, age 14.
- Joe was fully insured for Social Security purposes.

As Ill. 3.3 (Monthly Benefits If You Should Die in 1992) shows, Joe's dependents Kathy and Mary, will receive a total of approximately $1,598 per month for two years (until Mary reaches age 16). Kathy will receive $799 per month because Mary is under age 16. Mary's benefit is also $799 per month.

After Mary reaches age 16 and until she is age 18 (or age 19 if she's in high school), only Mary will receive benefits—approximately $799 per month.

When Kathy is age 65, she will receive approximately $1,065 monthly; or, if she elects to receive benefits at age 60, she will receive approximately $762.

Survivor Benefits—Example II

Let's consider another case—Steve Burns. Here is some information about him and his family:

- Steve is age 40 when he dies.
- He was earning $30,000 annually at the time of his death.
- His dependents include his surviving spouse, Susie, age 35 and two children—son, Jack, age 8 and daughter, Jan, age 12.
- Steve was fully insured for Social Security purposes.

Again using Ill. 3.3, we see that the maximum family monthly benefit (approximately $1,679) is payable to the family for six years (to Jan's age 18, when Jack is age 14). For the next two years, Susie and Jack will receive a total of $1,438 per month ($719 each). Then, after Jack reaches age 16, only he is entitled to benefits.

Beginning at age 65, Susie will receive widow's benefits of approximately $959 per month; or $686 monthly beginning at age 60, if she so elects. If Steve were only currently insured, Susie would not receive an old-age widow's benefit.

ILL. 3.3 ■ Monthly Benefits If You Die in 1992

Your Age in 1992	Who Receives Benefits	Your Present Annual Earnings				
		$12,000	$20,000	$30,000	$42,000	$55,500 and up
65	Spouse, age 65	$522	$ 722	$ 956	$1,037	$1,088
	Spouse, age 60	373	516	683	742	778
	Child; spouse caring for child	392	541	717	778	816
	Maximum family benefit	818	1,351	1,674	1,817	1,906
60	Spouse, age 65	518	714	941	1,027	1,076
	Spouse, age 60	370	510	672	734	769
	Child; spouse caring for child	388	535	705	770	807
	Maximum family benefit	805	1,338	1,646	1,797	1,882
55	Spouse, age 65	518	714	950	1,044	1,101
	Spouse, age 60	370	510	679	746	787
	Child; spouse caring for child	388	535	712	783	826
	Maximum family benefit	805	1,338	1,663	1,827	1,927
50	Spouse, age 65	518	714	957	1,065	1,135
	Spouse, age 60	370	510	684	762	812
	Child; spouse caring for child	388	535	718	799	851
	Maximum family benefit	805	1,338	1,676	1,864	1,987
45	Spouse, age 65	518	714	959	1,090	1,180
	Spouse, age 60	370	510	686	779	843
	Child; spouse caring for child	388	535	719	818	885
	Maximum family benefit	805	1,338	1,678	1,908	2,064
40	Spouse, age 65	518	714	959	1,103	1,227
	Spouse, age 60	370	511	686	789	877
	Child; spouse caring for child	388	536	719	827	920
	Maximum family benefit	806	1,339	1,679	1,931	2,147
35	Spouse, age 65	519	715	961	1,104	1,252
	Spouse, age 60	371	511	687	789	895
	Child; spouse caring for child	389	536	720	828	939
	Maximum family benefit	808	1,340	1,681	1,932	2,190
30	Spouse, age 65	521	719	966	1,108	1,269
	Spouse, age 60	372	514	691	792	907
	Child; spouse caring for child	391	539	725	831	952
	Maximum family benefit	814	1,345	1,691	1,939	2,221

Source: William M. Mercer, Incorporated

Retirements Benefits—Example I

An estimate of retirement benefits (PIA) at normal retirement age can be obtained by using another reference table in the *Guide*. Let's consider a third case so that you can practice using this type of Social Security table. Here are some facts about Jim Moore and his family:

- Jim's current age is 55.
- He presently is earning $42,000 per year.

ILL. 3.4 ■ Monthly Benefits At Age 65

Your Age in 1992	Who Receives Benefits	Your Present Annual Earnings				
		$12,000	$20,000	$30,000	$42,000	$55,500 and up
65	You	$522	$722	$956	$1,037	$1,088
	Spouse* or child	261	361	478	518	544
64	You	524	723	958	1,041	1,096
	Spouse* or child	262	361	479	520	548
63	You	516	712	944	1,029	1,085
	Spouse* or child	258	356	472	514	542
62	You	520	717	953	1,041	1,102
	Spouse* or child	260	358	476	520	551
61	You	521	718	955	1,047	1,112
	Spouse* or child	260	359	477	523	556
55	You	525	726	973	1,082	1,176
	Spouse* or child	262	363	486	541	588
50	You	499**	692**	924**	1,047**	1,158**
	Spouse or child	264	366	489	554	613
45	You	497**	689**	917**	1,050**	1,183**
	Spouse or child	266	369	491	562	633
40	You	501**	695**	921**	1,058**	1,208**
	Spouse or child	268	372	493	567	647
35	You	486**	676**	892**	1,026**	1,176**
	Spouse or child	270	375	495	570	653
30	You	471**	656**	863**	993**	1,139**
	Spouse or child	272	378	498	573	657

* Benefit at age 65 or at any age with eligible child under age 16 in care.

** These amounts are reduced for retirement at age 65 because the Normal Retirement Age (NRA) is higher for these persons; the reduction factors are different for the worker and the spouse.

Source: William M. Mercer, Incorporated

- His dependents include his wife, Martha, age 45, and daughter, Jean, age 2.
- Jim plans to retire at age 65, fully insured.

From Ill. 3.4 (Monthly Benefits at Age 65) we can determine that Jim's benefit at age 65 will be approximately $1,082 per month. At that time, his daughter, Jean, will be age 12 and will receive a monthly benefit of $541 until she is age 18 (or to age 19 if she's in high school). Martha also will receive a benefit of $541 per month for four years (until Jean is age 16).

When Martha reaches age 65 (age 62 for reduced benefits), she again will qualify for spousal benefits. As with survivor benefits, a maximum family benefit applies.

■ CHAPTER 3 QUESTIONS FOR REVIEW

1. Those excluded from Social Security coverage are:

   a. workers under age 25.
   b. all federal employees.
   c. employees covered by the Railroad Retirement system.
   d. anyone who works for a religious organization.

2. The Social Security "PIA" is the:

   a. "preferred indicated amount" which each covered person must choose.
   b. "primary insurance amount," received when the insured retires at the normal retirement age.
   c. benefits available to survivors if the insured dies before age 50.
   d. amount reached by indexing current earnings.

3. The amount payable under Social Security in case of disability, death or retirement is based on the:

   a. worker's AIME.
   b. size of the worker's PIA.
   c. size of the worker's family.
   d. amount that the worker's employer wants to contribute to the Social Security program.

4. If a person who is age 61 in 1992, earning $55,500 a year, retires at age 65, how much will he or she receive in Social Security payments?

   a. $556
   b. $1,102
   c. $1,112
   d. $1,176

5. The unmarried children of a deceased worker can receive benefits past the age of 18 only if they are:

   a. college students.
   b. living at home.
   c. working at least part-time.
   d. disabled.

4
Capital Utilization Method

T he capital utilization method of solving your clients' financial needs is explained in this chapter. You'll learn a step-by-step procedure in filling out the total needs work skeet. The three main ways to compute present requirements are discussed. The remaining steps to be taken to assure a successful sales presentation, including an outline of a family financial plan, are shown.

■ ■ ■ ■ ■

Two methods of meeting an individual's or family's total financial needs are examined in the next four chapters. Both methods involve creating capital through life insurance. However, they differ significantly in disposing of the capital.

The method discussed in this chapter is *capital utilization*. It refers to the technique of combining life insurance principal (proceeds) plus interest to supplement income from other sources. This is commonly done by using a policy's settlement options to liquidate the proceeds systematically, allowing both principal and interest to last as long as they are needed. This method is traditionally referred to as *programming*.

By contrast, the *capital retention* method utilizes only the interest or investment earnings generated by the principal; the principal is not liquidated. This technique is sometimes referred to as *capital need analysis*.

■ HISTORICAL DEVELOPMENT

Total needs selling and the capital utilization method of satisfying total needs were developed several decades ago in response to people's financial needs and circumstances. At that time, government and employee benefits were minimal (if provided at all). Confidence in the usual forms of savings and investments was very low because people still were very aware of the stock market crash, building and loan association closings, bank failures and other financial calamities of that period.

In that setting, programming became an ideal solution to financial needs created by death or retirement. In one plan it combined the total needs selling of life insurance with the capital utilization method of distributing the proceeds on a guaranteed, affordable basis. For relatively modest installment payments, an insured breadwinner was guaranteed:

1. specified amounts of cash and income for his or her family if the insured's death occurred before retirement;
2. lifetime retirement income if the insured lived to retirement and
3. cash or loan values or other optional values for emergencies or investment opportunities.

These guarantees were obtainable in no other way. Generally, less capital was needed to guarantee a given income by this method than to provide the same amount of nonguaranteed income from investment returns because yields were low at that time.

Today

Many changes have occurred since those early days of programming. Money is certainly more plentiful. Interest and yields of typical savings and investment media are much higher. Government and employee benefits are far more numerous. Family incomes are much higher and vastly more families have two incomes.

On the other hand, living standards and the costs of living also have increased. So have taxes . . . not only on what we earn and have while we're here, but also on what we leave when we die.

The certainties and guarantees of programming, with its capital utilization method of satisfying needs, are still available. The provision of a given amount of income still generally requires less capital under this plan than by any other means—and consequently may require less drain on current income.

When programming first came into its own, a family usually had only one breadwinner. Today it's not unusual to find family situations where both spouses are substantial producers of income for the family. To accommodate such situations, programming has evolved to encompass the financial impact generated by the loss of either spouse's income due to death or retirement.

■ THE BASIC CONCEPT

Programming is a composite of two elements: total needs fact-finding and life insurance. Fact-finding makes it possible to determine cash and income needs, any special needs or desires and present assets that may offset some of those needs. Life insurance provides an affordable means of immediately creating large amounts of capital at the insured's death or of accumulating needed capital if the insured lives to retirement.

However, the capital utilization method of *distributing* capital is the key to programming because it provides the means not only of determining how much capital is required to satisfy any given needs, but also of guaranteeing delivery of the capital exactly as specified. After cash needs are determined, the amount of capital needed to satisfy them is obvious. So the capital utilization method relates primarily to *income* needs. As noted earlier, each income installment consists of a combination of earnings and capital, actuarially determined, so the capital is depleted with the final guaranteed income installment.

In short, the basic capital utilization method employs the appropriate income settlement options in life insurance and/or annuity contracts to determine the capital required to make guaranteed distributions consistent with satisfying the income needs.

When To Use

The capital utilization method guarantees delivery of cash or income in the amount and at the time required by the plan. It is suitable for people of average financial means because it may be the only affordable way to do the job. It also is recommended for people with very conservative investment natures: people who intently follow the daily stock market quotations and are seriously disturbed whenever their holdings drop a few points.

The capital retention method, as we'll see in Chapter 6, makes no such guarantees and generally requires more capital than the capital utilization method to provide the same amount of income. Use of the capital utilization method, as opposed to the capital retention method, depends upon the particular family's financial circumstances, needs and temperament.

Assumptions

The following discussion is based upon the assumptions that you know:

1. how to use an adequate fact-finding tool;
2. the complete spectrum of available life insurance and annuity contracts and the mechanical details of applying for and servicing them;
3. the Social Security benefits as discussed in Chapter 3;
4. the general nature of group life insurance and employee retirement plans and
5. how to use tables of commonly used information, e.g., compound interest and discount (present value) tables, cash value and settlement option tables, mortgage amortization schedules and tax tables.

■ THREE MAIN STEPS IN THE SALES PROCESS

Fact-Finding

Phase one of the sales process is a thorough job of fact-finding. As we've discussed, this is the first major step in any total needs selling method. Moreover, the facts and information you obtain (except possibly for the extent of details) and the procedures followed are virtually identical in the capital utilization and capital retention methods.

Engineering the Plan

After you obtain the required facts and other pertinent information, you are ready for phase two: engineering a plan that satisfies the family's total needs. This phase consists of:

1. calculating the amount of new life insurance required to equal the difference between a family's total needs and the portion of those needs that present resources can satisfy;
2. selecting the particular life insurance contracts to recommend and
3. preparing the sales presentation.

Engineering a plan usually requires neither precise calculations nor extremely time-consuming considerations about how to use each particular policy. Detailed procedures are handled more efficiently after the sale. Keep procedures as simple as possible. Where you can round off figures, say to the nearest $100 for cash amounts, and to the nearest $5 or $10 for income amounts.

Also, use the same assumed factors whenever practical. For example, when projecting life insurance cash or income values as well as net earnings on invested capital, use a common interest or investment rate assumption. When actually working with prospects, the interest rate you use may depend upon what your prospects think is reasonable at the time. If you use computer printouts, you may wish to select current rates for illustrative purposes. In this text, we use 5 percent and 6 percent annual rates, realizing that you or your prospects may want to use a higher or lower net rate.

Remember, during phase two, don't be too precise and keep it simple.

Wrapping Up the Sale

Phase three, wrapping up the sale, consists of three major steps:

1. *Presentation and Closing*—presenting the total needs plan, including recommendations, to the prospect and closing the sale.
2. *Follow-through and Delivery*—preparing to deliver the new life insurance policies and then actually delivering them with an explanation and record of the new plan.
3. *Continuing Service*—periodically reviewing and updating the plan, including the sale of any additional insurance required to keep the plan current.

■ APPLYING THE PROCESS

Because the first major function of engineering the plan is calculating the amount of new life insurance required to satisfy all objectives of the plan, in determining those objectives, consider two basic situations: one-income and two-income families. For illustrative and discussion purposes, a sample total needs work sheet, representing a composite of similar forms, appears as Ill. 4.1 and Ill. 4.2.

The One-Income Family

As defined in this text, a *one-income family* may have one or both parents living in the household and at least one minor child (including an expected child). The method used to complete the work sheet is as follows:

1. The family with both parents present where one is the sole income producer and the other is responsible primarily for the home: Whether it is the husband or the wife who remains at home with the children, use the accompanying

ILL. 4.1 ■ Total Needs Work Sheet (side 1)

TOTAL NEEDS WORK SHEET

CASH NEEDS

If _____ Dies   If _____ Dies
(Husband)   (Wife)

	Objectives	S.S. and/or Other Govt. Benefits	Present Requirements	Objectives	S.S. and/or Other Govt. Benefits	Present Requirements
Final Expenses	$	$	$	$	$	$
Housing Fund						
Education Fund						
		TOTAL CASH NEEDS $			TOTAL CASH NEEDS $	

MONTHLY INCOME NEEDS

If _____ Dies   _____'s Age
(Husband)   (Wife)

☐ ☐ ☐ ☐ ☐ Life

	For ___ Depend. Yrs. While 3 or More Elig.	For ___ Depend. Yrs. While 2 Eligible	For ___ Depend. Yrs. While 1 Eligible	For ___ Yrs. Until Wife is Age ___	Wife for Life
Objectives	$	$	$	$	$
S. S. and/or Other Govt. Benefits					
Continuing Income (Wife)					
Present Requirements	$	$	$	$	$
	$	$	$	$	$

Capital Amounts
$ _____
_____
_____
_____
_____
$ _____

If _____ Dies   _____'s Age
(Wife)   (Husband)

☐ ☐ ☐ ☐ ☐ Life

	For ___ Depend. Yrs. While 3 or More Elig.	For ___ Depend. Yrs. While 2 Eligible	For ___ Depend. Yrs. While 1 Eligible	For ___ Yrs. Until Husband is Age ___	Husband for Life
Objectives	$	$	$	$	$
S. S. and/or Other Govt. Benefits					
Continuing Income (Husband)					
Present Requirements	$	$	$	$	$
	$	$	$	$	$

Capital Amounts
$ _____
_____
_____
_____
$ _____

TOTAL PRESENT REQUIREMENTS

If _____ Dies $ _____   If _____ Dies $ _____
(Husband)   (Wife)

Side 1

ILL. 4.2 ■ Total Needs Work Sheet (side 2)

PRESENT REQUIREMENTS vs. PRESENT RESOURCES

	If _____ Dies (Husband)	If _____ Dies (Wife)
Total Present Capital Requirements	$_____	$_____
Present Life Insurance Applicable	$_____	$_____
Other Present Asset Values Applicable	$_____	$_____
Total Present Capital Resources	$_____	$_____
New Life Insurance Required	$_____	$_____

NEW INSURANCE RECOMMENDED

On _____ $_____ _____ $____/____
　　(Husband)　(Amount)　　(Policy or Combination of Policies)　　(Premium)

On _____ $_____ _____ $____/____
　　(Wife)　　(Amount)　　(Policy or Combination of Policies)　　(Premium)

LIVING VALUES

RETIREMENT INCOME

For _____ at _____ AND _____ at _____ – _____
　　(Husband)　　(age)　　　　　(Wife)　　(age)　　(year)

From:

		Option or Earnings Rate	Monthly Life Income
Social Security and/or Other Gov't Benefits	_____ (Husband)		$_____
	_____ (Wife)		_____
Pension and/or Profit Sharing Plans	_____ (Husband)		_____
	_____ (Wife)		_____
Present Life Insurance	_____ (Husband)	(_____)	_____
	_____ (Wife)	(_____)	_____
New Life Insurance	_____ (Husband)	(_____)	_____
	_____ (Wife)	(_____)	_____
Other	_____		_____
	_____		_____
Total Monthly Retirement Income			$_____

MISCELLANEOUS (Education, Opportunity, Emergency Funds, etc.)

Side 2

work sheet and show each spouse's name in the appropriate space, completing the work sheet for each spouse.
2. The family with only one parent present as a result of death, divorce or other event: Because there is only one prospect to consider, complete only the part of the worksheet labeled either "husband" or "wife" whichever is applicable.

The Two-Income Family

Typically this family consists of a husband and wife and at least one minor child (including an expected child). In addition to their responsibilities as parents, both husband and wife work outside the home at income-producing jobs. So if either income stops for any reason, the total family income is likely to diminish substantially, especially when considering statistics indicating that a wife working full-time at an outside job accounts for as much as 40 percent or more of the family's income.

The accompanying work sheet is ideally suited to this situation. Enter the names of both husband and wife in the appropriate spaces and use the entire work sheet to establish what the situation would be if either breadwinner died.

■ STEP-BY-STEP PROCEDURES

The step-by-step work procedures involved in engineering the plan include determining (1) present requirements relative to cash needs, (2) present requirements relative to income needs, (3) present requirements relative to all needs and (4) present deficits.

Let's study each part of the work sheet and then in the next chapter we'll present some case illustrations.

Determine Present Requirements Relative to Cash Needs

First, you must determine the total capital amount presently required to satisfy all cash needs—after allowing for applicable Social Security and other government benefits—(1) if the husband should die and (2) if the wife should die. Those needs, as listed on the left of the work sheet, are final expenses, housing fund and education fund. This section of the work sheet, shown here as Ill. 4.3 is divided into two identical parts, one for each spouse. A common practice is to finish the analysis for one spouse, then complete it for the other. In a one-parent situation, simply complete the applicable part.

Objectives

The dollar objectives for the cash needs in the event of each spouse's death may be taken directly from the fact-finding form. However, the housing fund objective should go *only* on the income-producing spouse's side in a *one-income family* situation. For the *two-income family*, you may elect to divide the total amount of a mortgage between the two spouses in the same proportion that their individual incomes bear to their combined total income. A spouse producing 60 percent of the combined income, for example, would have a housing fund objective equal to 60 percent of the total mortgage; the other spouse would have a 40 percent objective. The rationale is that each working spouse is assuming this respective percentage of all family

ILL. 4.3 ■ Cash Needs

	If _____ Dies (Husband)			If_____ Dies (Wife)		
	Objectives	S.S. and/or Other Govt. Benefits	Present Requirements	Objectives	S.S. and/or Other Govt. Benefits	Present Requirements
Final Expenses	$	$	$	$	$	$
Housing Fund						
Education Fund						
	TOTAL CASH NEEDS $			TOTAL CASH NEEDS $		

expenditures and obligations, including the mortgage, while both spouses are living. So, if a spouse dies, the survivor simply will continue to provide his or her share.

If the family is currently renting its residence, funds to provide all or part of the purchase price of a home or the income to rent a home may be provided in the plan. As in the case of a mortgage, the percentage of the total objective to be provided can equal that spouse's percentage contribution to the combined family income.

The education fund objective generally should be recorded whenever a spouse's death will destroy the income being counted on for this purpose. This applies to both one-income and two-income families and should reflect the needs and objectives you determined during the fact-finding interview.

Social Security and/or Other Government Benefits

The fact-finding form should provide all information required to determine the amounts of Social Security and other government benefits, if any, applicable to each cash need for each spouse.

Present Requirements

After you have completed the other columns for each spouse, subtract the *Social Security and/or Other Govt. Benefits* (second column) from the *Objectives* (first column) and record the difference in the *Present Requirements* column on each side. The totals represent amounts presently required to satisfy all cash needs at each spouse's death. Note that, generally, there will be a total cash need requirement for each spouse, whether or not that spouse is an income producer.

Determine Present Requirements Relative to Income Needs

The purpose of the next section of the work sheet, shown as Ill. 4.4, is to determine the total capital amount presently required to satisfy all the *monthly income needs* of the surviving family. Among the factors to consider are:

1. the current capital or other financial resources—e.g., Social Security—that can be applied to reduce the amount that must be acquired to satisfy those needs;
2. the number of years each need will exist;
3. a factor that takes into account the possible impact of future inflation on those needs and

4. the present value of the capital amounts needed in the future.

Note that Ill. 4.4 is divided into two identical parts relating to the income needs of the surviving family members, regardless of which spouse dies. We will examine the top part as if actually applying it to a case. Assume the husband is either the sole or primary income producer.

ILL. 4.4 ■ Monthly Income Needs

If _____ Dies (Husband)   _____'s Age (Wife)   Life

	For ___ Depend. Yrs. While 3 or More Elig.	For ___ Depend. Yrs. While 2 Eligible	For ___ Depend. Yrs. While 1 Eligible	For ___ Yrs. Until Wife is Age ___	Wife for Life
Objectives	$	$	$	$	$
S. S. and/or Other Govt. Benefits					
Continuing Income (Wife)					
Present Requirements	$	$	$	$	$
Capital Amounts $ ___ ___ ___ ___ ___ $ ___					
	$	$	$	$	$

If _____ Dies (Wife)   _____'s Age (Husband)   Life

	For ___ Depend. Yrs. While 3 or More Elig.	For ___ Depend. Yrs. While 2 Eligible	For ___ Depend. Yrs. While 1 Eligible	For ___ Yrs. Until Husband is Age ___	Husband for Life
Objectives	$	$	$	$	$
S. S. and/or Other Govt. Benefits					
Continuing Income (Husband)					
Present Requirements	$	$	$	$	$
Capital Amounts $ ___ ___ ___ ___ ___ $ ___					
	$	$	$	$	$

TOTAL PRESENT REQUIREMENTS

If _____ Dies $ _____   If _____ Dies $ _____
(Husband)   (Wife)

Income Need Periods

Start by identifying the typical surviving family's income need periods if the husband should die. After writing in the actual names on the first two lines of the top part, follow these steps:

1. Record the wife's present age on the *Age* blank.
2. If there are three or more eligible family members—children under age 18 and/or a wife with a child under age 16 (or disabled) in her care—determine the number of years until two or less are eligible. Record that number in the heading of the first column and the wife's age at the end of that period in the blank box above the column. (If only two are eligible, go to the next step.)
3. Determine the number of years during which only two family members will be eligible, if appropriate. Record that number in the heading of the second column and the wife's age at the end of that period in the blank box above the column.
4. Determine the number of years during which there will be only one eligible family member (e.g., a child age 16–18). Record that number in the heading of the third column, and the wife's age at the end of that period in the box above the column.
5. Determine the number of years from the *youngest* child's age 18 until the wife's age 60 if she is *not* an income producer—or expected retirement age (age 62 or over) if she *is* an income producer. This is the *blackout period*, when *no* Social Security benefits are paid to the spouse. Record that number of years and her age at the end of that period in the fourth column.
6. The fifth column represents the period beginning at the widow's age as recorded in the preceding step and continuing for life; record that age again in the box above the column.

Completion of the preceding six steps will identify clearly the surviving family's income need periods and the duration of each. These periods are applicable in most one-income, as well as two-income, family situations.

Objectives

From the fact-finding form, ascertain the monthly income amounts needed during the income need periods and record those amounts in the *Objectives* line in the respective columns.

Social Security and/or Other Government Benefits

The next step is to determine the monthly income amounts of Social Security and/or other government benefits payable to the surviving spouse during the income need periods and to record them on line two in the income need period columns.

This applies to benefits attributable to either the deceased husband's coverage under a benefit plan or to the wife's own coverage under the plan. Generally, the *larger* (but not both benefits) may be taken when both spouses are covered under the same plan, e.g., at retirement when both are "fully insured" under Social Security.

Continuing Income

This step applies only if the surviving spouse is an income producer or has income from his or her own pension or other employee benefit plan. Record this monthly income amount on the third line in the appropriate columns.

Present Requirements

In this step, subtract both the government benefit and continuing income amounts from the objectives and record the results in each column.

Determine Capital Amounts

The amounts on the *Present Requirements* line are the *actual* additional amounts that will be needed *monthly* during each income period to raise the actual income to the amount needed. Here is how these monthly amounts can be turned into the exact amount of capital needed to produce these monthly amounts.

First, these monthly amounts must be translated into the *capital* needed to produce the monthly income. This is the amount required if the income is needed immediately. Then you must figure the *present value* of each of the capital amounts. Remember that most of these *Present Requirements* will not be needed until several years into the future. The farther into the future the need is, the smaller is the amount needed now to produce the income.

One definition of *present value* describes it as an amount that, if invested at an assumed rate of interest, will accumulate to a specified sum at a given future date. The process involves first determining the capital amount needed to provide the monthly income amount shown in each of the present requirement columns. That answer represents a *future* value—or how much will be needed to provide the desired monthly income listed in that column over a period of time beginning at some future date. Then, present value tables will show how much money is needed *today* to equal that answer for each column, considering future interest earnings on amounts that will remain in the fund until they're paid as income.

Here many life insurance agents add an additional factor to build some protection against continuing inflation. They work with the family to establish an expected annual inflation factor for each year from the present to the end of the income period. Then a present value, based on anticipated interest earnings, is established for that higher figure.

Finally, all of the amounts needed today to satisfy the income needs in all columns are totaled and the sum is the total fund needed today to satisfy *all* income needs.

There are three general ways to determine the total amount needed today to satisfy all present requirements using the capital utilization method: (1) the interest lay-back method, (2) the no-interest method and (3) the present value or discount method. The following discussion is a general overview of the first two methods. Then, we will take a detailed look at the present value or discount method.

Interest Lay-Back Method

The *interest lay-back* method was the original form of programming. Although it is rarely used, we'll describe it briefly since some people still have programs based on this method. You should have a general understanding of how those old programs were constructed before attempting to expand or replace them.

The interest lay-back method uses settlement options to determine how much capital, in terms of policy face amount, is required to produce the needed life income for the survivor after retirement. For the sake of simplicity, let's assume that the proceeds from a $100,000 policy will produce the needed $1,000 a month for the survivor from age 65 for an average life span of another 15 years. That $100,000, paid when the insured dies, is the starting point.

Let's assume that the insured dies at the age of 31. The $100,000 is held by the insuring company at 6 percent interest, waiting to do the job of providing that retirement income of $1,000 a month. Yearly interest of $6,000 is generated and that means that the survivor can receive $500 a month interest on the proceeds during the years before retirement.

This programming method then moves *back* to the previous income needs period, which in this case can be defined as the blackout period, when the survivor is no longer eligible for Social Security payments because there are no dependent children in the household. Assume the needed income in this period is $2,000 and the survivor takes home about $1,200 a month. In addition, add the $500 in monthly interest, which leaves a shortfall of $300 a month. Then, the amount of insurance proceeds needed to generate that extra $300 a month is figured and added to the original $100,000 face amount needed to produce retirement income.

The interest lay-back method continues to move *backward* through each income need period. If there is a gap between the income available from earnings, assets and life insurance proceeds at any point, the proceeds amount needed to produce the income is added to the face amount of insurance needed. The final capital amount to be produced by insurance coverage should cover *both* income needs throughout the survivor's working life, as well as the specific need for retirement income.

No-Interest Method

The *no-interest* method to determine the capital amount needed to provide monthly income does not include interest on proceeds being held—except when using a life income option.

In the no-interest method, as in both the interest lay-back and present value or discount methods, the income objective for each income period is entered on the *Objectives* line of the work sheet. Subtract the available benefits and continuing income and enter the income requirement, the extra amount needed on the *Present Requirements* line.

Then, just multiply the monthly amount needed times the number of *months* in the income period, and enter that figure in the *Capital Amounts* box. For instance, suppose a person needs an extra $100 a month for five years. Multiply $100 by 60 months ($5 \times 12$) for a capital amount of $6,000.

For the last income need period, the *For Life* column, use an appropriate life income option and the surviving spouse's age at the start of the period to determine the face amount required to produce the needed extra income for the period of time.

Proponents of this method credit it with several advantages:

1. It is simple, quick and readily adaptable to one-interview program selling.
2. By disregarding interest on proceeds, it helps to offset the rate of inflation.
3. It develops insurance needs that sufficiently approximate actual needs for planning purposes, especially when the future impact of inflation is uncertain.

Present Value or Discount Method

In this course, we will focus on the *present value* or *discount method* to determine monthly income needs. The present value or discount method uses a little more sophisticated mathematical procedure to determine the interest on proceeds held for later income. The need periods are taken up in the order in which they arise. The sales advantage is that the amounts required to satisfy one or more early income need periods can be determined readily if the prospect doesn't buy the whole program immediately. Computerized programming generally utilizes this method. The fact-finding input cards and printout proposal forms may look a little different, but the technique is basically the same.

■ STEP-BY-STEP THROUGH THE PRESENT VALUE METHOD

Let's walk through a present value computation. The steps are numbered and keyed to Ill. 4.5, the sample work sheet.

Determine Cash Needs

The first needs to record are cash needs. These are the one-time needs that arise at death. In the *Objectives* column **(1)**, write the amounts that the prospects listed on the fact-finding form. They include *final expenses*, *housing fund* and *education fund*.

In the next column **(2)** list any benefits that are available. These will include benefits such as Social Security or veteran's death benefits. *Subtract* the benefits available from the amount needed in the *Objectives* column to find the *Present Requirements* **(3)** in each category. Add the numbers in the *Present Requirements* column for the total cash needs.

Determine Monthly Income Needs

Income needs are ongoing. Prospects have estimated these income needs on the fact-finding form.

The present value method is based on the assumption that money *requirements* and fund *availability* will vary with the size of the family. The work sheet has five income need periods, ending with the spouse's income need for life.

The First Income Period

The first income period **(4)** starts at the surviving spouse's present age and is defined by the number of dependents still at home. If there are two or more children below the age of 16, use the first column labeled *While three or more eligible*. If there is only one child at home, use the next column labeled *While two eligible*. Write the surviving spouse's present age in the box at the top of the first column.

ILL. 4.5 ■ Total Needs Work Sheet

TOTAL NEEDS WORK SHEET

CASH NEEDS

If _____ Dies   If _____ Dies
(Husband)   (Wife)

	Objectives	S.S. and/or Other Govt. Benefits	Present Requirements	Objectives	S.S. and/or Other Govt. Benefits	Present Requirements
Final Expenses	$ *1*	$ *2*	$ *3*	$	$	$
Housing Fund						
Education Fund						

TOTAL CASH NEEDS $ _____   TOTAL CASH NEEDS $ _____

MONTHLY INCOME NEEDS

If _____ Dies   _____'s Age
(Husband)   (Wife)

	35 For *8* Depend. Yrs. While 3 or More Elig.	**43** For *1* Depend. Yrs. While 2 Eligible	**44** For *1* Depend. Yrs While 1 Eligible	**46** For *14* Yrs. Until Wife is Age *60*	**60** Wife for Life / Life
Objectives	$ *4*	$ *5*	$ *6*	$ *7*	$ *8*
S. S. and/or Other Govt. Benefits					
Continuing Income (Wife)					
Present Requirements	$	$	$	$	$
	$	$	$	$	$

Capital Amounts
$ _____
3,000
$ _____

How long will Social Security benefits for these dependents last before they change? Let's use an example to illustrate: a 35-year-old mother left with two children, ages 10 and 7. Let's assume they are eligible for the maximum family benefit until the oldest child reaches age 18.

The surviving parent's age is 35. Write that number in the box just above the first column (**4**). In the caption to the first column, record the number of dependent years until the oldest child reaches age 18. Write "8" in the blank provided.

Objectives: On the first line, write the monthly income needed. This information is normally found in the fact finder that you prepared during your presentation with the prospect.

S.S. and/or Other Govt. Benefits: Using the Social Security table in the text, find the amount of Social Security benefits available to survivors.

Continuing Income (Wife): Next, list any continuing income from the spouse's employment.

Present Requirements: The *Social Security* and *Continuing Income* lines reflect funds that are available. The top line, *Objectives*, reflects the monthly income figure, the money that is needed. Subtract *Social Security* and *Continuing Income* from the *Objectives* to determine the *Present Requirements* for the first income period.

The Second Income Period

Now that the needs for the first eight-year income period are completed, the oldest child is now 18 and ineligible for Social Security benefits. In the second income period **(5)**, the mother, now age 43 and remaining child, now age 15, are each eligible to receive an individual benefit for another year (until the second child reaches age 16). Add eight years to the surviving parent's age in the first income period $(8 + 35 = 43)$. That is the number to write in the box above the second income period. Write "1" in the blank provided in the caption above the second column to indicate the number of dependent years.

Objectives: Once again, the objectives can be found in the fact finder. Enter the monthly income needs for the second income period.

S.S. and/or Other Govt. Benefits: Social Security benefits change after the first eight years because the oldest child is now 18.

Continuing Income (Wife): List any continuing income from the spouse's employment.

Present Requirements: Subtract *Social Security* and *Continuing Income* from the *Objectives* to determine the *Present Requirements* for the second income period.

The Third Income Period

When the second child reaches age 16, more benefits are lost. The child receives benefits until age 18, but the "parent" benefit is gone. Another income need period has started **(6)**. Record the mother's age at *that* point $(35 + 8 + 1 = 44)$ and write "2" in the "dependent years" blank. Fill in the spaces for *Objectives, S.S. and/or Other Govt. Benefits, Continuing Income (Wife)* and *Present Requirements* as explained above.

The Fourth Income Period

When the second child reaches age 18, the blackout period **(7)** begins for the surviving parent. This means that no Social Security benefits are payable until retirement at age 60 or 65. The length of this income need period should be indicated on the work sheet, e.g., $60 - 46 = 14$ years.

The Fifth Income Period

Finally, the "life income" **(8)** column is reached. It is the age when the surviving parent expects to retire. In this instance let's assume a retirement age of 60.

What's Still Needed

The first line, *Objectives* is the estimated *need* for funds. The second *S.S. and/or Other Govt. Benefits* and third lines are available funds. Subtract benefits and earned income from the estimated need. There probably will be a shortfall that's likely to increase as the income need periods move toward retirement. How can we meet this need?

Determine Capital Amounts

We now have the amount *per month* that will be needed in each income period and *how long* it will be needed. How can that be translated to the *capital amounts* that will produce this income?

First, refer to the "Fixed Period (Amount) Option Table" in Chapter 5 (Ill. 5.19) to find out how much money is needed to produce monthly income. Shown here is the amount needed to produce a set amount of monthly income, ranging from $10 to $150, for a specified number of years. For instance, let's say the individual in our "income period" example needs an additional $200 a month for the third income period—the two years in which only the second child is receiving benefits. Illustration 5.19 shows us that $234 is needed to provide $10 a month for two years. To find out how much is needed to provide $200 a month, first we divide $200 by 10 to get $20. Then, multiply $20 × $234 to get $4,680.

Remember that this amount will not be needed for nine years into the plan (eight years in the first income period and one year in the second). What *present value* is needed to produce this amount in nine years? This step gives the system its name. In Chapter 5, Ill. 5.20 shows a Present Value (Discount) Table. It gives the present value of $1 for a specified number of years into the future at various interest rates.

We'll assume a 5 percent interest rate. The present value of a dollar nine years in the future is .6446. That means that to produce $1 nine years from now, you must invest about 64 ½ cents at 5 percent now. So, we multiply the capital needed, $4,680, by, .6446 and come up with $3,016.72 or about $3000. In other words, $3,000 deposited today at 5 percent interest will grow to $4,680 in nine years. The $4,680 will then provide the needed $200 a month for two years, the duration of the third income period.

In Ill. 4.5, write this amount on the third line in the *Capital Amounts* box. The capital amount needed for the other income periods would be determined the same way. Each line corresponds to each income period. The final income period uses the life income option table (see Ill. 5.21) that furnishes the amount required to provide $10 monthly life income at various ages. In the case studies, we use the last column of that table "20 years certain and life" for the last income period capital amount. The steps for determining each specific income period are demonstrated in the case studies in Chapter 5.

Determine Present Requirements Relative to All Needs

This step simply sums up the total amount presently required to satisfy all *cash* needs and the total capital amount presently required to satisfy all *income* needs. The totals should be recorded appropriately in the *Total Present Requirements* section at the bottom of the work sheet illustrated here as Ill. 4.6.

Determine Present Deficits

This step also is simple if you did a good job of fact-finding. In the next section, side two of the work sheet, the total amount of applicable present resources is sub-

ILL. 4.6 ■ Present Requirements

If _____ Dies $ _____   If _____ Dies $ _____
     (Husband)   (Wife)

tracted from the *Total Present Requirements* if either spouse should die, to determine the total present capital deficit in each event (see Ill. 4.7).

When determining the resources available to a spouse, include *all* proceeds payable
to the spouse from present life insurance on the other spouse's life—but *only* the
present liquidation value of general assets that the spouse reasonably can count on
for cash or income purposes.

For example, include only the minimum amounts of cash and savings that generally
are maintained. The equity in a residence (market value less mortgage) usually
should not be included if the home is to be retained or replaced with another owned
residence. The present net liquidation values of such assets as personal property,
business interests and investments (real estate, stocks, bonds, etc.) should be included only to the extent they would be liquidated or could produce a reasonable
percentage of income if retained.

Include any presently vested values in the deceased spouse's pension or profit-sharing plans and any other relatively sure cash or liquidation values that would be available. Record the totals in the appropriate spaces on the work sheet. After you
determine how much new life insurance is needed on the life of each spouse, select
the contracts to recommend and prepare your presentation.

See the step-by-step explanation of this process in Ill. 4.8.

Select and Record the Contracts

No matter what method you used to determine the *amounts* of insurance needed, the
specific kind of policy—or combination of policies—to recommend on each
spouse's life must now be decided.

In the fact-finding discussion, you probably obtained either a definite premium commitment or a clear picture of the prospect's capacity to pay. In addition, you probably discussed ideas relative to such living objectives as retirement goals and
educational opportunities for the children. While discussing present insurance, you
probably got a good idea of the prospect's feelings about various types of policies.

There's no single procedure for selecting the right policies. To a great extent it's a
matter of applying good judgment and common sense to the information and impressions obtained in fact-finding. Your goal normally is to provide the total face
amount of new life insurance required, plus as much as possible of the living values
desired, for the available premium dollars; in other words, to select life insurance
contracts that will do the best job.

If a choice must be made between providing the total amount of new life insurance
required and more favorable living values, the former usually is the better choice.

ILL. 4.7 ■ Present Requirements vs. Present Resources

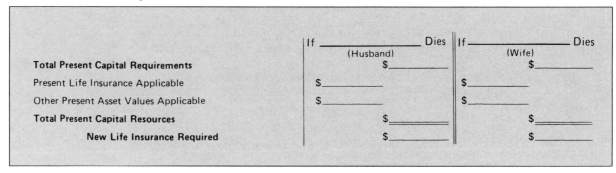

	If _____ Dies (Husband)	If _____ Dies (Wife)
Total Present Capital Requirements	$_____	$_____
Present Life Insurance Applicable	$_____	$_____
Other Present Asset Values Applicable	$_____	$_____
Total Present Capital Resources	$_____	$_____
New Life Insurance Required	$_____	$_____

There probably is considerable time left to build living values but there may be little or no time to create the capital needed to satisfy family objectives if a spouse dies.

Here are some additional considerations when deciding what policies to present:

- If you must sell term insurance, stress the value of converting to permanent insurance in the future.
- Don't underestimate the prospect's ability to pay. Sometimes it's best to start a little high to prevent this possibility. You always can present an alternate plan with a lower premium, if necessary.
- Recommend reducing term insurance cautiously. If it is used (other than possibly to satisfy such objectives as dependency period income or mortgage insurance needs), the amount of coverage may drop below the level needed to satisfy the prospect's needs.

Record Policy Selections

To avoid having possibly to repeat the selection process, record key identifying information on the work sheet immediately (see Ill. 4.9.)

Record Pertinent Living Values

The policy selection process also includes considerations of the new insurance's living values, especially how they relate to the prospect's living objectives and present values. Record those considerations on the work sheet, so they readily will be available when you prepare the sales presentation (see Ill. 4.10).

■ PREPARE THE SALES PRESENTATION

Your final task is to prepare the sales presentation. This involves compiling and organizing pertinent information and recommendations into a sales kit and presenting it in the most effective and motivating manner.

In one-interview program selling, preparation must be very quick and smooth—almost automatic. Simplified forms and tools designed for that purpose are available. When the two-interview system is used, preparations can be more elaborate and detailed.

ILL. 4.8 ■ Capital Utilization Step-by-Step Procedures

CAPITAL UTILIZATION
The Present Value or Discount Method

Step 1. Determine cash needs from fact-finding.

    a. Objectives:
            Final Expenses
            Housing Fund
            Education Fund
                minus
    b. Social Security and/or Other Govt. Benefits
                equals
    c. Present Requirements, for money to meet cash needs at death

Step 2. Identify the different income need periods, based on the surviving spouse's age and number of dependent children.

    a. First Income Period—starts at the surviving spouse's present age and is defined by the number of dependents still at home. If there are two or more children below age 16, use the first column (*While three or more eligible*); if there is only one child at home use the next column (*While two eligible*), etc.
    b. Second Income Period—starts when first child no longer receives Social Security benefits; only surviving spouse and remaining child(ren) receive benefits.
    c. Third Income Period—starts when youngest child turns 16.
    d. Fourth Income Period—starts when youngest (and last eligible) child turns 18; this begins the blackout period for the surviving spouse.
    e. Fifth Income Period—starts at the surviving spouse's retirement.

Step 3. Determine income needs for each income period, using fact-finding form and *Guide to Social Security*.

    a. Objectives (the income needed for each income period)
                minus
    b. Social Security and/or Other Govt. Benefits payable during each income period
                minus
    c. Continuing Income to be received during each income period
                equals
    d. Present Requirements, the additional monthly income needed to meet that period's objectives

Step 4. Convert the Present Requirement income needs into Capital Amounts that will produce this income for each period.

    a. First Income Period—amount necessary today to generate the additional income needed for the duration of the first income period, given a specified rate of return. Use Ill. 5.19. Enter this amount on the first line in the *Capital Amounts* box.
    b. Remaining Income Periods—amount necessary to have on hand in the future to generate the additional income needed for the duration of each remaining income period. Use Ill. 5.19 to determine the amount necessary to provide each period's income; then use Ill. 5.20 to discount those sums and determine their present value. (Note: for any single income period that extends for life, use Ill. 5.21 instead of 5.19.) Enter these amounts on the second and subsequent lines in the *Capital Amounts* box.

ILL. 4.8 ■ Capital Utilization Step-by-Step Procedures (continued)

Step 5. Determine *all* cash and income (capital) needs.

    a. Total Cash Needs for final expenses, housing fund and education fund
       plus
    b. Capital Amounts from all income periods
       equals
    c. Total Present Requirements

Step 6. Determine present deficit

    a. Total Present Requirements
       minus
    b. Present Life Insurance
       minus
    c. Other Present Asset Values
       equals
    d. NEW LIFE INSURANCE NEEDED

Among the items you'll need in the sales kit are:

1. the original fact-finding form, including notes regarding the prospect's objectives;
2. a simple outline highlighting the application of present resources against objectives and revealing the deficits (new insurance required) if either spouse should die;
3. a summary of the key benefits of the recommended policies;
4. application blanks for each spouse, including any necessary supplemental forms and
5. letters giving you the authority to act as the prospect's representative in servicing any present policies.

An Effective Program Outline

To be effective, the outline of the proposed program must highlight (1) the objectives; (2) how much present resources offset those objectives and (3) how much is still needed to satisfy them completely. Abbreviated highlights of the recommended new insurance and the amount of retirement income are also included.

The "Family Financial Summary," the outline presentation form shown as Ill. 4.11, has been used effectively by many life insurance agents. Note that it includes all elements previously mentioned, relates to needs arising in the event of either spouse's death and accommodates either a one-income or a two-income family situation.

ILL. 4.9 ■ New Insurance Recommended

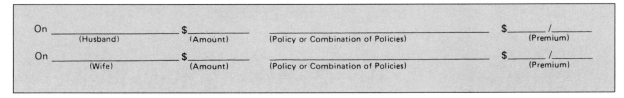

ILL. 4.10 ■ Living Values

RETIREMENT INCOME

For _____ at _____ AND _____ at _____ — _____
     (Husband)   (age)   (Wife)   (age)   (year)

From:
                                                                             Monthly
                                                                         Life Income

Social Security and/or Other Gov't Benefits   _____ $_____
                                          (Husband)
                                    _____   _____
                                        (Wife)

Pension and/or Profit Sharing Plans   _____   _____
                                        (Husband)
                                    _____   Option or   _____
                                        (Wife)   Earnings Rate

Present Life Insurance   _____ (_____)   _____
                                        (Husband)
                                    _____ (_____)   _____
                                        (Wife)

New Life Insurance   _____ (_____)   _____
                                        (Husband)
                                    _____ (_____)   _____
                                        (Wife)

Other   _____   _____
                                   _____   _____

           Total Monthly Retirement Income $_____

MISCELLANEOUS (Education, Opportunity, Emergency Funds, etc.)

The outline depicts the *results*—not the details—of the recommended plan. And because results are what the prospect will want and will buy, the outline provides the basis for a highly effective and motivating sales presentation.

■ CHAPTER 4 QUESTIONS FOR REVIEW

1. Engineering the plan consists of all of the following, EXCEPT:

   a. preparing the sales presentation.
   b. approaching the capital utilization prospect.
   c. calculating the amount of new life insurance needed.
   d. selecting life policies to recommend.

2. In the no-interest method of capital utilization, the monthly amount needed is multiplied by:

   a. the number of years in the income period.
   b. the number of months in the income period.
   c. a discount factor keyed to the recipient's age.
   d. None of the above.

ILL. 4.11 ■ Family Financial Summary

PREPARED FOR:_____   DATE:_____

FAMILY FINANCIAL SUMMARY

	For _____ if (Wife) _____ should die. (Husband)	For _____ if (Husband) _____ should die. (Wife)
CASH NEEDS		
Final Expenses – Objective	$_____	$_____
Less Social Security and/or Other Govt. Benefits	$_____	$_____
Present Requirement	$_____	$_____
Your Housing Fund – Present Requirement	$_____	$_____
Your Children's Education – Objective	$_____	$_____
Less Social Security and/or Other Govt. Benefits	$_____	$_____
Present Requirement	$_____	$_____
Total Cash Needs	$_____	$_____
MONTHLY INCOME NEEDS		
Dependency Period – 3 or more eligible – Objective	$_____	$_____
Less Social Security and/or Other Govt. Benefits	$_____	$_____
Less Continuing Personal Income	$_____	$_____
Present Requirement (Income–Capital)	$_____ – $_____	$_____ – $_____
Dependency Period – 2 eligible – Objective	$_____	$_____
Less Social Security and/or Other Govt. Benefits	$_____	$_____
Less Continuing Personal Income	$_____	$_____
Present Requirement (Income–Capital)	$_____ – $_____	$_____ – $_____
Dependency Period – 1 eligible – Objective	$_____	$_____
Less Social Security and/or Other Govt. Benefits	$_____	$_____
Less Continuing Personal Income	$_____	$_____
Present Requirement (Income–Capital)	$_____ – $_____	$_____ – $_____
For spouse (no children) – Objective	$_____	$_____
– to Age _____	_____	_____
Less Continuing Personal Income	$_____	$_____
Present Requirement (Income–Capital)	$_____ – $_____	$_____ – $_____
For spouse (no children) – Objective	$_____	$_____
– for Life After Age _____	_____	_____
Less Social Security and/or Other Govt. Benefits	$_____	$_____
Less Continuing Personal Income	$_____	$_____
Present Requirement (Income–Capital)	$_____ – $_____	$_____ – $_____
Total Capital to Satisfy Income Needs	$_____	$_____
Total Capital to Satisfy Cash and Income Needs	$_____	$_____
Less Existing Life Insurance and Other Assets	$_____	$_____
Amount Still Required to Satisfy Your Objectives	$_____	$_____

RECOMMENDATIONS:

RETIREMENT INCOME if you live, starting at _____ 's age _____ and _____ 's age _____:
(Husband)   (Wife)

From Social Security and/or Other Government Benefit Plans . . . . $_____

From Present Insurance, Employee Retirement Plans, and Other Resources . . . . $_____

From Recommended New Life Insurance . . . . $_____

Total Retirement Income . . . . $_____

3. The *Present Requirement* for each income period can be found by:

   a. adding together the monthly income figure and Social Security payments and subtracting continuing income.
   b. adding Social Security payments and continuing income and subtracting the Present Requirement from that figure.
   c. subtracting both Social Security payments and continuing income from the monthly income figure.
   d. adding Social Security, Present Requirement and continuing income.

4. The blackout period starts when the:

   a. surviving spouse retires.
   b. oldest child leaves home.
   c. youngest child turns 18.
   d. youngest child turns 16.

5. The sales advantage of the present value method is that:

   a. everyone can afford coverage under this method.
   b. the amount required for one or more of the early income periods can be determined readily if the prospect doesn't buy the whole program immediately.
   c. since the system works "back to front," the prospect can be sure that retirement needs will be met.
   d. the system is simple and easy to use.

5

Capital Utilization Case Studies

I n this chapter we'll apply the capital utilization method of total needs selling to realistic family situations. You'll become more familiar with the information to be entered on the fact-finding form and translating that information to the work sheet. We'll complete the work sheet, make policy selections and prepare presentation forms for each of two case studies.

■ ■ ■ ■ ■

We examined the capital utilization method of total needs selling (programming) and discussed policy selection and preparation of the sales presentation and the sales kit in Chapter 4. This chapter presents case studies of one-income and two-income family situations.

■ A ONE-INCOME FAMILY CASE

You have completed a thorough fact-finding session with Arnold and Brenda Jones. You now wish to engineer a total needs plan. Arnold is the family's sole income producer; he and Brenda have two school-age children. Other facts about the Jones family follow.

Family Data

Arnold—Age 35; good health; employed as assistant personnel manager for Beta Corporation

Brenda—Age 30; good health; not employed outside the home

Children—Connie, age 9 and David, age 4; both are healthy

General Financial Data

Arnold—$42,000 annual salary ($3,500 per month) plans to work to age 65

Brenda—Not employed outside the home; no future plans to become employed

Present General Assets—$1,500 cash and checking account; $1,500 in U.S. Savings Bonds; $2,000 in stocks and mutual funds; $16,000 vested in Beta's pension plan; presently no other general assets that would be liquidated or would produce income at either spouse's death

Present Liabilities—$41,105 mortgage on home; $1,000 in other loans

Present Life Insurance

Arnold—$100,000 Group (term); $29,000 Term to 65; $15,000 Whole Life purchased at age 26; $5,000 paid-up 20-Pay Life (purchased by parents at Arnold's birth)

Brenda—No coverage

Children—$2,000 Whole Life on each

Social Security*

Arnold—Fully insured; current family death benefit of about $1,932; age-65 retirement benefit of about $1,026 (reduced for early retirement) in today's dollars; $255 single-sum death benefit

Brenda—No coverage

Other Data

Veteran's Death Benefit—Arnold is eligible for $150 single-sum death benefit

Pension and Profit-Sharing Plans—Arnold is covered by a plan that will pay about $800 per month in addition to Social Security at age 65

Additional Premium—The Joneses could set aside an additional $100 per month, if needed

Objectives

Arnold and Brenda's objectives are shown in Ill. 5.1.

■ THE WORK SHEET FOR ARNOLD AND BRENDA JONES

The present value method of programming is used in the work sheet illustrations that follow because it is both widely used and the basis for most computer methods. The Social Security figures used are for illustration purposes only. For current figures, refer to the latest edition of the *Guide to Social Security*.

---

* Assumes 1992 Social Security rates.

ILL. 5.1 ■ Objectives for Arnold and Brenda Jones

Objectives	If Arnold Dies	If Brenda Dies
Cash Needs:		
Final Expenses*	$15,000	$15,000
Housing Fund	41,105	—
Education Fund	40,000	—
Monthly Income Needs:		
Dependency Period Income:		
Until *Connie* is age 18	$ 2,000/mo	$ 3,500/mo
Until *David* is age 16	1,800/mo	3,500/mo
Until *David* is age 18	1,800/mo	3,500/mo
Spouse's Life Income:		
To *Brenda* to age 60	$ 1,200/mo	
For life thereafter	1,200/mo	
To *Arnold* to age 65		$ 3,500/mo
For life thereafter		1,700/mo
Retirement income at Arnold's age 65 if both live	$2,500/mo (in terms of today's dollars or current purchasing power)	

*Although the couple felt that most final expenses might be a little higher for Arnold, they included a much larger amount of "Other" in this term and much higher "Income" objectives if Brenda dies. These undoubtedly reflect awareness of such hidden costs as replacing the child-care and housekeeping services if Brenda should die.

Cash Needs

The *Cash Needs* section of the work sheet is shown as Ill. 5.2. The objectives for both spouses came directly from the fact-finding form. The $405 in the second column on the *Final Expenses* line is the $255 lump-sum Social Security death benefit plus the $150 death expense reimbursements for a veteran from the Veteran's Administration.

ILL. 5.2 ■ Cash Needs

If **Arnold** Dies (Husband)   If **Brenda** Dies (Wife)

	Objectives	S.S. and/or Other Govt. Benefits	Present Requirements	Objectives	S.S. and/or Other Govt. Benefits	Present Requirements
Final Expenses	$ 15,000	$ 405	$ 14,595	$ 15,000	$	$ 15,000
Housing Fund	41,105	—	41,105			
Education Fund	40,000	—	40,000			
TOTAL CASH NEEDS			$ 95,700	TOTAL CASH NEEDS		$ 15,000

The void in the second column opposite *Education Fund* reflects the elimination of student benefits from Social Security for all who were not eligible for the benefits before September 1, 1981, and in postsecondary schools before May 1982.

The third column for each spouse is the balance remaining when the second column is subtracted from the first, with the total at the bottom.

Monthly Income Needs (In Terms of Income)

The income periods and column heads in the next section of the work sheet, illustrated as Ill. 5.3, should clearly identify the surviving spouse's age and the number of years (or lifetime) covered. They are derived easily from the fact-finding information and entered at the top of the columns for each spouse.

Note that the income objectives reflect the percentages suggested in the fact finder, plus, in case of Brenda's death, higher objectives to cover the hidden costs of replacing the child-care and housekeeping services that she currently performs. Here, except in the final column, the objectives in the event of Brenda's death are equal to Arnold's continuing income.

The next line in the upper part of this section indicates the Social Security benefits payable during the three periods prior to the youngest child's age 18 and the lifetime period after Brenda's age 60.

Because Brenda has no continuing income and does not plan to become an income producer, there are no entries on that line in the upper part of this section.

In the lower part, Arnold's continuing income is entered in each of the first four periods. His age-65 Social Security benefit and his pension plan income *plus* retirement income from his present life insurance are entered in the last column. All income objectives and amounts are based on today's dollars. Arnold's age-65 benefit is a reduced benefit because, beginning in 2003, "normal retirement age" rises gradually from age 65 to age 67.

The entries on the *Present Requirements* line of the upper and lower parts of this section are the balances remaining after subtracting the second and third lines from the *Objectives* line. As you can see from Ill. 5.3, Arnold would have no present income requirements if Brenda were to die; his continuing income during his working years, and then his pension plus Social Security benefits during his retirement years, would provide the income he needs. However, if Arnold were to die, the situation changes radically as Brenda has a present income requirement during each income period. Let's take a look at how Brenda's income requirements could be met.

Monthly Income Needs (Capital Amounts)

The next step is to convert the income needed for each period into capital amounts that, invested at a given rate, can generate the income Brenda will need for those periods. To do this, we will use three financial tables, which are included at the end of this chapter. The "Fixed Period (Amount) Option Table" (Ill. 5.19) and the "Life Income Option Table" (Ill. 5.21) are life insurance settlement option tables, based on a 3 percent rate. The "Present Value (Discount) Table" (Ill. 5.20), which shows the present value (P.V.) of $1 at the end of various numbers of years, is also based on a 3 percent rate. This is a conservative interest rate assumption since most companies

ILL. 5.3 ■ Monthly Income Needs (Income)

MONTHLY INCOME NEEDS

If _Arnold_ Dies
(Husband)

Brenda 's Age
(Wife)

30	39	42	44	50	Life
For _9_ Depend. Yrs. While 3 or More Elig.	For _3_ Depend. Yrs. While 2 Eligible	For _2_ Depend. Yrs. While 1 Eligible	For _16_ Yrs. Until Wife is Age _60_	Wife for Life	

	30	39	42	44	50
Objectives	$ 2,000	$ 1,800	$ 1,800	$ 1,200	$ 1,200
S. S. and/or Other Govt. Benefits	1,932	1,656	828	—	789
Continuing Income (Wife)	—	—	—	—	—
Present Requirements	$ 68	$ 144	$ 972	$ 1,200	$ 411

If _Brenda_ Dies
(Wife)

Arnold 's Age
(Husband)

35	44	47	49	65	Life
For _9_ Depend. Yrs. While 3 or More Elig.	For _3_ Depend. Yrs. While 2 Eligible	For _2_ Depend. Yrs. While 1 Eligible	For _16_ Yrs. Until Husband is Age _65_	Husband for Life	

	35	44	47	49	65
Objectives	$ 3,500	$ 3,500	$ 3,500	$ 3,500	$ 1,700
S. S. and/or Other Govt. Benefits	—	—	—	—	1,026
Continuing Income (Husband)	3,500	3,500	3,500	3,500	800
Present Requirements	$ —	$ —	$ —	$ —	$ —

TOTAL PRESENT REQUIREMENTS

If _____ Dies $ _____
(Husband)

If _____ Dies $ _____
(Wife)

are paying more than the 3 percent minimum guarantee; however, this conservative approach allows us to round the capital amounts, as precision is unnecessary.

Using the present value or discount method, we have computed Brenda's present requirements in amount of capital, as shown in Ill. 5.4. Let's review the steps we used.

Starting with the first income period, which begins now at Brenda's age 30 and continues for nine years until she is 39, we determined that the income need is $68 a month. If we look at the "Fixed Period (Amount) Option Table" (Ill. 5.19), we see that it takes $950 (at 3 percent) to provide $10 per month for nine years. To determine what it would take to provide $68 a month for nine years, we use the formula: $68 ÷ $10 × $950. This equals $6,460 or rounded, $6,500—the amount needed today to produce $68 a month for nine years. This amount is written on the first line in the *Capital Amounts* box of Ill. 5.4. This amount is the present value (P.V.) because the income starts immediately.

In the second income period, $144 a month is needed for three years. We again refer to Ill. 5.19 and see that it takes $345 to provide $10 a month for three years; therefore, we apply the formula to determine the capital needed to generate $144 a month for the same period: $144 ÷ 10 × $345 = $4,968. However, this $4,968 will not be needed until the end of the first income period, which is nine years from now. Thus, we have to determine an amount necessary today (the present value) that will grow to $4,968 in nine years. For this, we refer to Ill. 5.20, "Present Value (Discount) Table." As this illustration shows, the P.V. of $1 at the end of nine years is $.7664.

ILL. 5.4 ■ Monthly Income Needs (Capital Amounts)

If _Arnold_ Dies (Husband)   _Brenda_'s Age (Wife)

Ages: 30   37   41   44   60   Life

	For 9 Depend. Yrs While 3 or More Elig	For 3 Depend. Yrs While 2 Eligible	For 2 Depend. Yrs While 1 Eligible	For 16 Yrs. Until Wife is Age 60	Wife for Life
Objectives	$2,000	$1,800	$1,800	$1,200	$1,200
S. S. and/or Other Govt. Benefits	1,932	1,656	828	—	789
Continuing Income (Wife)	—	—	—	—	—
Present Requirements	$68	$144	$972	$1,200	$411

Capital Amounts —
$6,500
3,800
16,000
121,500
35,800
$183,600

So, the present value of $4,968 at the end of nine years can be calculated as $.7664 × $4,968 = $3,807, or $3,800 rounded, as shown on the second line in the *Capital Amounts* box.

In the third income period $972 a month is needed for two years. We see from Ill. 5.19 that it takes $234 to provide $10 monthly for two years; therefore, to generate $972 monthly for two years it will take $972 ÷ 10 × $234 = $22,745. Again, this amount will not be needed until the end of the second period, or twelve years from now. Illustration 5.20 shows the P.V. of $1 at the end of twelve years is $.7014; therefore, the P.V. of $22,745 at the end of twelve years is $.7014 × $22,745 = $15,953. Rounded, that's $16,000, as shown in the *Capital Amounts* box.

For the fourth income period ($1,200 a month for 16 years), Ill. 5.19 shows that it takes $1,532 to provide $10 per month for 16 years. The amount needed to generate $1,200 a month for this same period is $1,200 ÷ 10 × $1,532 = $183,840. This $183,840 will be held to the end of the first three periods, or 14 years, before it's needed. The P.V. of $1 at the end of 14 years is $.6611; that means the P.V. of $183,840 at the end of 14 years is $.6611 × $183,840 = $121,537. Rounded, that's $121,500, as shown on the fourth line.

In the last income period, we bring a new factor to our calculation. During this period, the objective is to provide $411 a month, beginning at Brenda's age 60, for the remainder of her *life*. Thus, we need the help of an annuity table, like the "Life Income Option Table" (see Ill. 5.21). As this table shows, it would take $2,114 to provide $10 per month for life (with 20 years certain), beginning at Brenda's age 60. Thus, to generate $411 a month for life at age 60, it would take $411 ÷ 10 × $2,114 = $86,885. However, this amount will not be needed until the end of the fourth period, or 30 years. We again refer to Ill. 5.20, and see that the P.V. of $1 at the end of 30 years is $.4120; thus, the P.V. of $86,885 at the end of 30 years is $.4120 ×

ILL. 5.5 ■ Total Present Requirements

TOTAL PRESENT REQUIREMENTS

If *Arnold* Dies $ *279,300*
(Husband)

If *Brenda* Dies $ *15,000*
(Wife)

$86,885 = $35,796. Rounded, this is $35,800 and is shown on the fifth line in the *Capital Amounts* box.

The total of the capital amounts of Ill. 5.4 equals $183,600. That's the total capital required (by the present value method) to provide all of Brenda's present income requirements. The sum of this amount and the *Cash Need* amount of $95,700 determined in the first section (see Ill. 5.2) is the *Total Present Requirements* in terms of capital amounts if Arnold dies, as shown in Ill. 5.5.

New Life Insurance Required

The next simple, but very important, step is determining the amount of new life insurance required on each spouse. Use the work sheet section shown in Ill. 5.6 as a guide. After writing the name of each spouse at the head of each column, *first* enter on each side the respective *Total Present Capital Requirement* for each spouse. *Second*, enter the applicable amounts of present insurance on the spouse's life. These may come directly from the fact-finding form. *Third*, enter the total of the liquid assets available to each surviving spouse, based on the fact-finding information previously obtained. *Fourth*, total the life insurance and other liquid assets. The final entries are the remainders when the fourth lines are subtracted from the first lines in the columns.

Those final entries are probably the most important figures in the entire case study. They represent the amounts of new life insurance required on the life of each spouse if the objectives are going to be satisfied. In this case, $109,300 of new life insurance is required on Arnold and $10,000 is required on Brenda.

New Life Insurance Recommended

When it comes to recommending new life insurance, use good judgment and common sense. Many kinds of policies and combinations of policies are available. What

ILL. 5.6 ■ Present Requirements vs. Present Resources

	If *Arnold* Dies (Husband)	If *Brenda* Dies (Wife)
Total Present Capital Requirements	$ *279,300*	$ *15,000*
Present Life Insurance Applicable	$ *149,000*	$ *—*
Other Present Asset Values Applicable	$ *21,000*	$ *5,000*
Total Present Capital Resources	$ *170,000*	$ *5,000*
New Life Insurance Required	$ *109,300*	$ *10,000*

ILL. 5.7 ■ New Insurance Recommended

On *Arnold* $*109,300*   *$50,000 WL + $59,300 10-yr. term* $ *88.75 / mo*
(Husband)   (Amount)   (Policy or Combination of Policies)   (Premium)

On *Brenda* $*10,000*   *WL with WP* $ *11.25 / mo*
(Wife)   (Amount)   (Policy or Combination of Policies)   (Premium)

are the best selections? What contracts should you recommend and why? To help answer these questions, let's review the information that relates to this decision.

Helpful data and impressions gained from the fact-finding session indicate that the Joneses:

- can put an additional $100 per month into the plan if necessary.
- consider living values important. They want funds for their children's education and about $2,500 per month (today's dollars) for retirement (about 71 percent of salary) at age 65.
- are frugal. They are buying their home and life insurance for Arnold and the children, are maintaining very little other indebtedness as well as saving and are investing some money.
- believe in whole life insurance. They bought it for Arnold, even with considerable group coverage in force, and for the children.
- have a good income and a promising future. Arnold is a second-level manager and probably will receive promotions and substantial salary increases during the next five to ten years.

Based on that information, let's select the policies for the Jones family. There may be several other good selections; however, the important point is to base the final selection upon in-depth consideration of the couple's needs, circumstances, attitudes and desires.

First, we'll cover all protection needs, aiming for additional premiums not to exceed about $100 per month.

Second, we'll make as much of that coverage as possible (within the premium limit) whole life because this is what the couple prefers. Other clients may need and want the newer interest rate sensitive or adjustable life products. Consider these policies if they are in your portfolio. Whole life, however, is our choice here. It builds good living values, education and opportunity funds, retirement income, paid-up insurance and other benefits.

Third, if permanent insurance can't provide the entire amount of protection needed (without exceeding the premium limit), we'll mix it with a convertible, renewable ten-year, level-term policy or rider. It will provide a lot of pure protection per premium dollar now and keep the door open for more cash value insurance if things go well during the next ten years.

ILL. 5.8 ■ Living Values Retirement Income

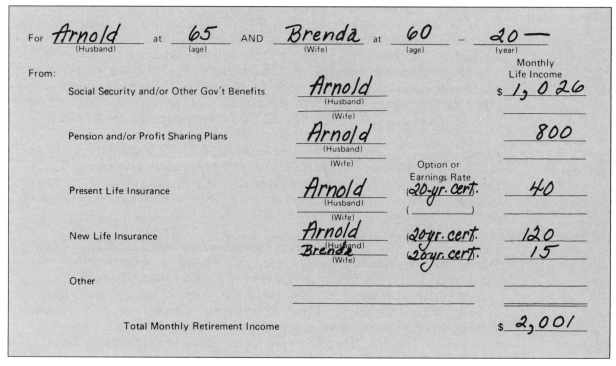

For **Arnold** (Husband) at **65** (age) AND **Brenda** (Wife) at **60** – **20—** (year)

From:

			Monthly Life Income
Social Security and/or Other Gov't Benefits	**Arnold** (Husband)		$ **1,026**
	(Wife)		
Pension and/or Profit Sharing Plans	**Arnold** (Husband)		**800**
	(Wife)	Option or Earnings Rate	
Present Life Insurance	**Arnold** (Husband)	(**20-yr. cert.** ( )	**40**
	(Wife)		
New Life Insurance	**Arnold** (Husband)	(**20 yr. cert.**	**120**
	Brenda (Wife)	(**20 yr. cert.**	**15**
Other			
Total Monthly Retirement Income			$ **2,001**

That's our strategy; let's implement it. To determine how much premium we have to work with for Arnold's coverage, let's take care of Brenda's required coverage first.*

Total monthly premium available	$100.00
Brenda: $10,000 Whole Life with W. P., monthly premium	$ 11.25
Arnold: $50,000 Whole Life with W. P., monthly premium	$ 61.00
plus $59,300 ten-year level-term rider with W. P., convertible and renewable, monthly premium	$ 27.75
Total monthly premium for Arnold's coverage	$ 88.75
Total monthly premium for Arnold and Brenda's coverages	$100.00

Record these premium amounts in the next section of the work sheet, as illustrated in Ill. 5.7.

Living Values

Now let's consider some of the "living values" that will accrue in Arnold and Brenda's plan. These include cash values at the children's college ages, retirement income values and maybe some paid-up insurance at retirement. Let's look first at the retirement income, referring to the *Living Values* section of the work sheet, shown as Ill. 5.8.

---

* The rates and values used here and elsewhere throughout the remainder of the text are for *illustration* only. They serve our purpose of demonstrating methods and procedures. Be sure to use your own company's rates and values in real cases.

From fact-finding, we know that Arnold's Social Security PIA and benefits based upon it will be about $1,026 if he retires early at age 65 — based on his current salary of $42,000—in today's dollars. Note that normal retirement age rises beginning in the year 2003. (See the *Guide to Social Security*.) If Arnold waits until normal retirement age, his benefit will be higher. When Arnold reaches age 65, Brenda will only be age 60 and ineligible for a retirement benefit. At age 62, she will be entitled to a benefit, based on Arnold's earnings record, equal to 37.5 percent of Arnold's PIA. (The 37.5 percent amount will be reduced beginning in the year 2003.) If she waits until normal retirement age, her benefit will be one-half of Arnold's PIA.

Arnold's pension is presently scheduled to pay $800 for life starting at age 65. His existing whole life policy will provide a monthly life income of about $40. The new $50,000 whole life policy recommended on Arnold's life will provide about $120 monthly life income (20-year certain) at age 65. The new insurance on Brenda will provide $15 a month.

Totaling the foregoing entries results in a retirement income of about $2,001 per month—based on today's pay and benefit levels—subject to some possible variations noted under the *Miscellaneous* section of the work sheet. Although this amount falls short of the $2,500 objective, this is no immediate problem for three reasons. First, as their finances improve, Arnold can convert all or part of the term coverage to whole life. Second, at age 62, Brenda will be eligible for Social Security retirement benefits. Third, they have 30 years to build additional retirement values to meet the shortfall and offset inflation.

Because both spouses will need a final expense fund after retirement, as well as before, let's recommend that they retain two policies as paid-up insurance at that time: $5,000 on Arnold and $3,800 on Brenda. Those amounts, plus any other assets, owned then, would be available for final expenses after retirement.

They also indicated strong interest in educational opportunities for their children. As mentioned earlier Social Security will not provide education funds. This insurance program provides $40,000 of education funds for the children if Arnold dies. But what if he lives? Illustration 5.9 shows the cash values that would be available at

ILL. 5.9 ■ Cash Values Available at Each Child's Age 18

	At Connie's Age 18	At David's Age 18
Approximate cash or loan value of—		
Arnold's present $15,000 WL	$ 3,000	$ 3,900
Arnold's present $5,000 20-Pay Life	2,700	2,920
Arnold's new $50,000 WL	5,500	9,500
Brenda's new $10,000 WL	740	1,390
Other liquid assets (estimate)	5,000	5,000
Total cash available	$16,940	$22,710

each child's age 18. This information should be listed in the *Miscellaneous* section of the work sheet.

Capital Utilization—How To Determine Capital Amounts

The text examples use settlement option tables based on a 3 percent rate and a compound interest (discount) table that shows the present value of $1 at the end of the various numbers of years, also based on a 3 percent rate.

A Quick Review

The concept is easy. Here are the steps:

1. Determine the present requirements for all income periods.
2. Using the "Fixed Period (Amount) Option Table" (Ill. 5.19), find the number of years in the first income period. Then, multiply that figure with the present requirement (be sure to place a decimal point in the present requirement number). Write the answer in the first line in the *Capital Amounts* box.
3. For the second income period, repeat step 2 using the numbers for the second income period. Then, using the dependent years from the first income period, go to the "Present Value (Discount) Table" (Ill. 5.20). Multiply the P.V. of $1 by the sum of the fixed period (amount) option equation you have just determined. Write the answer in the second line in the *Capital Amounts* box.
4. For the third income period, add the dependent years from the first and second income periods. Then repeat step 3 above, writing the answers in the succeeding line in the *Capital Amounts* box.
5. Repeat step 4 for the fourth income period.
6. In the last income period, use the "Life Income Option Table" in Ill. 5.21, for 20-years certain and life. Then determine the P.V.

The Completed Work Sheet

The sample work sheet completed for both Arnold and Brenda is shown as Ill. 5.10. All that remains in this "engineering the plan" phase is to gather and organize the materials in the sales kit and to plan how that material will be presented in the actual sales presentation. As noted earlier, there are simplified kits that may be used in noncomplex situations on a one-interview basis. However the following discussion concentrates on the process as if it were a two-interview sale because (1) basic principles are the same in both techniques; (2) discussion of more extensive preparations are applicable to both simple and complex cases; (3) many life insurance agents prefer the two-interview system of programming and (4) our case study is a two-interview selling situation.

■ SALES KIT

Earlier, we discussed the key items that are to be included in the sales kit. Prepared kits frequently combine some of the standard items, especially the kits designed for use in one-interview program selling. Let's discuss those items as they are included in proper order in the sales kit.

ILL. 5.10 ■ Total Needs Work Sheet (side 1)

TOTAL NEEDS WORK SHEET

CASH NEEDS

If _Arnold_ Dies (Husband)   If _Brenda_ Dies (Wife)

	Objectives	S. S. and/or Other Govt. Benefits	Present Requirements	Objectives	S.S. and/or Other Govt. Benefits	Present Requirements
Final Expenses	$15,000	$405	$14,595	$15,000	$	$15,000
Housing Fund	41,105	—	41,105			
Education Fund	40,000	—	40,000			
	TOTAL CASH NEEDS		$95,700	TOTAL CASH NEEDS		$15,000

MONTHLY INCOME NEEDS

If _Arnold_ Dies (Husband)   _Brenda_'s Age (Wife)

30 9 39 3 42 2 44 16 60 Life

	For 9 Depend. Yrs. While 3 or More Elig	For 3 Depend. Yrs. While 2 Eligible	For 2 Depend. Yrs. While 1 Eligible	For 16 Yrs. Until Wife is Age 60	Wife for Life
Objectives	$2,000	$1,800	$1,800	$1,200	$1,200
S. S. and/or Other Govt. Benefits	1,932	1,656	828	—	789
Continuing Income (Wife)	—	—	—	—	—
Present Requirements	$68	$144	$972	$1,200	$411
	$	$	$	$	$

Capital Amounts
$ 6,500
3,800
16,000
121,500
35,800
$183,600

If _Brenda_ Dies (Wife)   _Arnold_'s Age (Husband)

35 9 44 3 47 2 49 16 65 Life

	For 9 Depend. Yrs. While 3 or More Elig.	For 3 Depend. Yrs. While 2 Eligible	For 2 Depend. Yrs. While 1 Eligible	For 16 Yrs. Until Husband is Age 65	Husband for Life
Objectives	$3,500	$3,500	$3,500	$3,500	$1,700
S. S. and/or Other Govt. Benefits	—	—	—	—	1,026
Continuing Income (Husband)	3,500	3,500	3,500	3,500	800
Present Requirements	$ —	$ —	$ —	$ —	$ —
	$	$	$	$	$

Capital Amounts
$
—
—
—
—
$

TOTAL PRESENT REQUIREMENTS

If _Arnold_ Dies $279,300 (Husband)   If _Brenda_ Dies $15,000 (Wife)

Side 1

ILL. 5.10 ■ Total Needs Work Sheet (side 2)

PRESENT REQUIREMENTS vs. PRESENT RESOURCES

If _Arnold_ Dies   If _Brenda_ Dies
(Husband)   (Wife)

	If Arnold Dies	If Brenda Dies
Total Present Capital Requirements	$ 279,300	$ 15,000
Present Life Insurance Applicable	$ 149,000	$ —
Other Present Asset Values Applicable	$ 21,000	$ 5,000
Total Present Capital Resources	$ 170,000	$ 5,000
New Life Insurance Required	$ 109,300	$ 10,000

NEW INSURANCE RECOMMENDED

On _Arnold_ $ _109,300_ $50,000 WL #59,300 10-yr. Term $ 88.75 / mo
   (Husband)   (Amount)   (Policy or Combination of Policies)   (Premium)

On _Brenda_ $ _10,000_   WL with WP $ 11.25 / mo
   (Wife)   (Amount)   (Policy or Combination of Policies)   (Premium)

LIVING VALUES

RETIREMENT INCOME

For _Arnold_ at _65_ AND _Brenda_ at _60_ – _20–_
   (Husband)   (age)   (Wife)   (age)   (year)

From:

		Option or Earnings Rate	Monthly Life Income
Social Security and/or Other Gov't Benefits	Arnold (Husband)		$ 1,026
	_____ (Wife)		
Pension and/or Profit Sharing Plans	Arnold (Husband)		800
	_____ (Wife)		
Present Life Insurance	Arnold (Husband)	(20-yr. cert.)	40
	_____ (Wife)	(_____)	
New Life Insurance	Arnold (Husband)	(20-yr. cert.)	120
	Brenda (Wife)	(20-yr. cert.)	15
Other	_____		
	_____		
	Total Monthly Retirement Income		$ 2,001 *

MISCELLANEOUS (Education, Opportunity, Emergency Funds, etc.)

* 1. In addition to above retirement income, there would be $5,000 paid-up ins. on Arnold, $3,800 on Brenda, and any other assets not used previously — or additional retirement income, if preferred.

2. If needed for education purposes, there would be approximately:
— $16,940 at Connie's age 18 or
— $22,710 at David's age 18 or
— $11,355 at Connie's age 18 and $11,355 at David's age 18

(Any of these values must be repaid or replaced, of course, if retirement values are to stand.)

Side 2

Original Fact-Finding Form

After preliminary greetings and remarks, open the presentation by reviewing the prospects' objectives as recorded on the original fact-finding form. After the prospects again have acknowledged these as their objectives (accepted the problem as their own), move into a presentation of their current financial situation relative to those objectives.

Outline Presentation

The second item in the sales kit is the completed outline presentation form. Everything on the "Family Financial Summary" is entered from the work sheet just completed. Noting the asterisk opposite *Total Monthly Retirement Income* and the living benefit entries in *Miscellaneous* on the work sheet be sure to cover these items. Pinpoint mathematical accuracy is not necessary. You're simply using the form to help the prospects recognize the current deficits in meeting their objectives. *This is the key to the sale.* The "Family Financial Summary" for Arnold and Brenda is shown in Ill. 5.11.

Recommendations and Key Benefits Sheet

This sheet can be a form or a tailor-made presentation for the individual situation. It should:

1. clearly identify the new policy or policies recommended on each spouse's life, including any special features and show the premiums;
2. show a breakdown of retirement income provided by the present resources, new insurance recommended and total proposed program;
3. state any recommendations relative to paid-up insurance after retirement and
4. indicate any living values available from present resources, recommended new insurance and total recommended plan.

A "Recommendations and Key Benefits" sheet prepared for the Joneses is shown as Ill. 5.12. Again, most of the information comes directly from the work sheet.

Sales Wrap-Up Forms

The remaining items in the sales kit are the forms you'll require (1) to submit the applications for new insurance and (2) to provide needed service on *present* insurance.

Now that the sales kit is complete and organized, you are prepared for the closing interview session. You are offering a sound, affordable plan for satisfying objectives and professional servicing of that plan; therefore, you have maximized your chances of making the sale—and of building a lasting client-agent relationship.

■ A TWO-INCOME FAMILY CASE

We have completed a detailed case study of engineering a total needs plan for the one-income family situation. Now let's engineer a plan for a two-income family but in much less detail because the procedures are virtually identical.

Assume we have just completed a fact-finding session with Bill and Nancy Smith for whom we now wish to engineer a total needs plan. The pertinent facts follow.

ILL. 5.11 ■ Family Financial Summary

PREPARED FOR: *Arnold & Brenda*　　　　　　DATE: *1/6*

FAMILY FINANCIAL SUMMARY

	For *Brenda* (Wife) if *Arnold* (Husband) should die.		For *Arnold* (Husband) if *Brenda* (Wife) should die.	
CASH NEEDS				
Final Expenses　Objective	$*15,000*		$*15,000*	
Less Social Security and/or Other Govt. Benefits	$ *405*		$ *—*	
Present Requirement		$*14,595*		$*15,000*
Your Housing Fund — Present Requirement		$*41,105*		$ *—*
Your Children's Education — Objective	$*40,000*		$ *—*	
Less Social Security and/or Other Govt. Benefits	$ *—*		$ *—*	
Present Requirement		$*40,000*		$ *—*
Total Cash Needs		$*95,700*		$*15,000*
MONTHLY INCOME NEEDS				
Dependency Period — 3 or more eligible — Objective	$*2,000*		$*3,500*	
Less Social Security and/or Other Govt. Benefits	$*1,932*		$ *—*	
Less Continuing Personal Income	$ *—*		$*3,500*	
Present Requirement (Income—Capital)	$ *68*	– $*6,500*	$ *—*	– $ *—*
Dependency Period — 2 eligible — Objective	$*1,800*		$*3,500*	
Less Social Security and/or Other Govt. Benefits	$*1,656*		$ *—*	
Less Continuing Personal Income	$ *—*		$*3,500*	
Present Requirement (Income—Capital)	$ *144*	– $*3,800*	$ *—*	– $ *—*
Dependency Period — 1 eligible — Objective	$*1,800*		$*3,500*	
Less Social Security and/or Other Govt. Benefits	$ *828*		$ *—*	
Less Continuing Personal Income	$ *—*		$*3,500*	
Present Requirement (Income—Capital)	$*972*	– $*16,000*	$ *—*	– $ *—*
For spouse (no children) — Objective	$*1,200*		$*3,500*	
— to Age	*60*		*65*	
Less Continuing Personal Income	$ *—*		$*3,500*	
Present Requirement (Income—Capital)	$*1,200*	– $*121,500*	$ *—*	– $ *—*
For spouse (no children) — Objective	$*1,200*		$*1,700*	
— for Life After Age	*60*		*65*	
Less Social Security and/or Other Govt. Benefits	$ *789*		$*1,026*	
Less Continuing Personal Income	$ *—*		$ *800*	
Present Requirement (Income—Capital)	$ *411*	– $*35,800*	$ *—*	– $ *—*
Total Capital to Satisfy Income Needs		$*183,600*		$ *—*
Total Capital to Satisfy Cash and Income Needs		$*279,300*		$*15,000*
Less Existing Life Insurance and Other Assets		$*170,000*		$*5,000*
Amount Still Required to Satisfy Your Objectives		$*109,300*		$*10,000*

RECOMMENDATIONS:

New Life Insurance of:
$109,300 on Arnold — $50,000 WL + $59,300 10-yr. term　$88.75/mo
$10,000 on Brenda — WL with WP　　　　　　　　　　　11.25/mo
　　　　　　　　　　　　　　　　　　　　　　　　　　——————
　　　　　　　　　　　　　　　　　　　　　　　　　$100.00/mo

RETIREMENT INCOME if you live, starting at *Arnold* (Husband) 's age *65* and *Brenda* (Wife) 's age *60*:

From Social Security and/or Other Government Benefit Plans	$ *1,026*
From Present Insurance, Employee Retirement Plans and Other Resources	$ *840*
From Recommended New Life Insurance	$ *135*
Total Retirement Income	$ *2,001*

ILL. 5.12 ■ Recommendations and Key Benefits

A. POLICY RECOMMENDATIONS

To provide the additional capital required to satisfy your family financial objectives completely if either of you should not live, it is recommended that you purchase additional life insurance as follows:

On Arnold's life—

$50,000 Whole Life with Disability Waiver of Premium	Monthly Premium	$ 61.00
$59,300 Ten-Year Term Rider (Convertible and Renewable) with Disability Waiver of Premium	Monthly Premium	$ 27.75
$109,300 New Capital Needed	New Monthly Premium	$ 88.75

On Brenda's life—

$10,000 Whole Life with Disability Waiver of Premium	Monthly Premium	$ 11.25
	Total New Monthly Premium	$100.00

B. RETIREMENT INCOME

If the recommended program is adopted, your combined monthly retirement income at Arnold's age 65 and Nancy's age 63 will be as follows:

From Arnold's Social Security coverage	$1,026
From Arnold's present insurance and pension plan	840
From Arnold's recommended new life insurance	120
From Brenda's recommended new life insurance	15
Total combined monthly retirement income	$2,001*

*In addition, there will be a $5,000 paid-up policy on Arnold and a $3,800 paid-up policy on Brenda—to cover final expenses that will occur sometime, even after retirement. If needed when the time comes, however, additional retirement income may be obtained from these policies also. Any other assets will be available to supplement the above, as well.

C. EDUCATION FUNDS

Under this plan substantial funds clearly have been provided for the education of Connie and David in the event of Arnold's death. But what if you both live? In that event, the recommended program will make education funds available as follows:

	At Connie's Age 18		At David's Age 18
From loans on present insurance†	$ 5,700	OR	$ 6,820
From loans on new insurance†	6,240	OR	10,890
From other liquid assets (estimate)	5,000	OR	5,000
Total funds available	16,940	OR	22,710
OR—by dividing the funds equally	$11,355	AND	$11,355

†Any insurance loan values used for educational purposes must be repaid or replaced, of course, if the above retirement income is to be available.

Family Data

Bill—Age 35; good health; employed as an accountant for ABC Company; assumes about 25 percent of housekeeping chores

Nancy—Age 35; good health; employed as a buyer at the POQ Department Store; assumes about 50 percent of housekeeping chores (remaining 25 percent of housekeeping chores handled by hired help)

Children — Susan, is age 9 and Tad, age 4; both are healthy

General Financial Data

Bill—$30,000 annual salary ($2,500 per month); plans to work to age 65

Nancy—$20,000 annual salary ($1,667 per month); plans to work to age 65 combined annual salary of $50,000 or $4,167 per month

Present General Assets—$2,000 cash and checking account; $6,000 in savings and other liquid assets

Present Liabilities—$30,000 mortgage; $2,200 in other loans

Present Life Insurance

Bill—$31,600 Group (term); $5,000 Whole Life purchased at age 26

Nancy—$26,600 Group (term); $2,000 paid-up 20-Pay Life (purchased by parents at her age 4)

Children—$2,000 Whole Life on each

Social Security*

Bill—Fully insured; present credited earnings would produce current family death benefit of $1,681; projected credited earnings to age 65 would produce an age-65 retirement benefit of $892 (reduced for early retirement) in today's dollars; $255 single-sum death benefit

Nancy—Fully insured; present credited earnings would produce a current family death benefit of $1,340; projected credited earnings to age 65 would produce an age-65 retirement benefit of $676 (reduced for early retirement) in today's dollars

---

* Assumes 1992 Social Security rates.

ILL. 5.13 ■ Objectives for Bill and Nancy Smith

Objectives	If Bill Dies	If Nancy Dies
Cash Needs:		
Final Expenses	$11,000	$11,000
Housing Fund*	18,000 (60%)	12,000 (40%)
Education Fund	40,000	40,000
Monthly Income Needs:		
Dependency Period Income:†		
Until *Susan* is age 18	$ 3,500/mo	$ 3,750/mo
Until *Tad* is age 16	3,500/mo	3,750/mo
Until *Tad* is age 18	3,000/mo	3,750/mo
Spouse's Life Income:		
To *Nancy* to age 60	$ 2,000/mo	
For life thereafter	1,500/mo	
To *Bill* to age 65		$ 2,500/mo
For life thereafter		1,500/mo
Retirement income at Bill's age 65 if both live	$2,500/mo (in terms of today's dollars or current purchasing power)	

*Responsibility for the mortgage is divided between the spouses in the approximate ratios as their respective incomes bear to their combined income (60%/40%).

†The higher income amounts needed if Nancy dies reflect the greater percentage of housekeeping chores she assumes and, consequently, the higher hidden costs to replace those services.

Other Data

Pension and Profit-Sharing Plans—Bill's company pension at 65 will be $245 a month; Nancy's company pension at age 65 will be $195 a month

Additional Premium—The Smiths could set aside an additional $150 per month, if needed

Objectives

The Smiths' cash and income objectives are shown in Ill. 5.13.

■ THE WORK SHEET FOR BILL AND NANCY SMITH

Based on the foregoing information, let's review the completed work sheet, shown as Ill. 5.14, using the present value method. Consider the following:

1. In this case, as in any case with two income-earners, it is important to note what happens to a surviving spouse's Social Security death benefit if he or she continues to work. Social Security imposes an "earnings limit"; any amounts earned over this limit (currently $7,440 a year) will cause a deduction in Social Security benefits. The Social Security benefits entered for both

Bill and Nancy in the income periods prior to the youngest child's age 18 were calculated to reflect the reduced benefits, because both earn over the allowable amount. These benefits were determined as follows:

In the event of Bill's death:
a. The first income period—Both children are eligible for $720 of monthly benefits ($720 × 2 = $1,440). Nancy is also eligible for a survivor benefit, but it will be reduced $1 for ever $2 she earns over the $7,440 limit. The reduction is determined in this way: $20,000 (annual income) – $7,440 (allowable earnings) = $12,560 (excess). The total benefit reduction is $12,560 ÷ $2 = $6,280. The monthly benefit reduction is calculated by dividing that sum by 12: $6,280 ÷ 12 = $523. That figure is subtracted from the monthly benefits payable to Nancy: $720 – $523 = $197. That amount, added to the benefit payable to the children, is $197 + $1,440 = $1,637.
b. The second income period—Only Nancy and Tad are eligible for Social Security benefits during this period, since Susan is now 18. The total benefit for the period is $197 + $720 = $917.
c. The third income period—Because Tad is over 16 now, Nancy is no longer eligible for Social Security benefits. Tad, however, will continue to receive $720 a month for two years, until he is 18.

In the event of Nancy's death:
a. The first income period—Both children are eligible for $536 of monthly benefits ($536 × 2 = $1,072). Bill is not eligible to receive any benefit since his current earnings are $30,000—$22,560 in excess of the current earnings limitation. His total benefit will be reduced by $11,280, or $940 a month, which totally offsets his $536 monthly benefit. Thus, the monthly Social Security benefit for the first period is $1,072.
b. The second income period—Only Tad will receive a benefit, since Susan is now 18 and Bill's benefit is offset. The monthly benefit for this period, which will extend for five years (until Tad is 18) is $536.

2. The Social Security benefit payable to Nancy after age 65 in the *Monthly Income Needs* section is the surviving spouse's benefit based on Bill's coverage because it is larger than her own age-65 retirement benefit. Bill's own age-65 Social Security retirement benefit also is used because it is larger than his benefit based on Nancy's coverage (see the *Guide to Social Security*).
3. The income requirements are converted to capital amounts by the present value or discount method, as explained earlier in this chapter.
4. Under the section *New Insurance Recommended*, coverage was split between whole life and ten-year convertible level term. Ideally, only whole life would have been used for two reasons: (a) prior purchases of whole life indicate an appreciation for this type of plan and (b) the cash surrender values could have been used to supplement retirement income. However, the $150 per month limit on additional premiums requires that ten-year convertible term be used in combination with whole life. (You may wish to use the newer interest rate sensitive or adjustable life products for additional flexibility.)
5. The Social Security retirement benefits are based on each spouse's own coverage because that total is more than either income-earner's combined husband-wife benefit.
6. The total monthly retirement income falls short of the $2,500 objective if both Bill and Nancy live to age 65. However, as their financial situation

ILL. 5.14 ■ Total Needs Work Sheet (side 1)

TOTAL NEEDS WORK SHEET

CASH NEEDS

If __Bill__ Dies (Husband)   If __Nancy__ Dies (Wife)

	Objectives	S.S. and/or Other Govt. Benefits	Present Requirements	Objectives	S.S. and/or Other Govt. Benefits	Present Requirements
Final Expenses	$11,000	$255	$10,745	$11,000	$255	$10,745
Housing Fund	18,000	—	18,000	12,000	—	12,000
Education Fund	40,000	—	40,000	40,000	—	40,000
TOTAL CASH NEEDS			$68,745			$62,745

MONTHLY INCOME NEEDS

If __Bill__ Dies (Husband)   __Nancy__'s Age (Wife)

	35 — For 9 Depend. Yrs While 3 or More Elig.	44 — For 3 Depend Yrs While 2 Eligible	47 — For 2 Depend. Yrs While 1 Eligible	49 — For 16 Yrs. Until Wife is Age 65	65 — Wife for Life / Life
Objectives	$3,500	$3,500	$3,000	$2,000	$1,500
S.S. and/or Other Govt. Benefits	1,637	917	720	—	961
Continuing Income (Wife)	1,667	1,667	1,667	1,667	195
Present Requirements	$196	$916	$613	$333	$344

Capital Amounts: $18,600 / 24,200 / 10,100 / 33,700 / 28,300 / $114,900

If __Nancy__ Dies (Wife)   __Bill__'s Age (Husband)

	☐ 35 — For ___ Depend Yrs While 3 or More Elig	44 — For 9 Depend Yrs While 2 Eligible	49 — For 5 Depend. Yrs While 1 Eligible	65 — For 16 Yrs. Until Husband is Age 65	Husband for Life / Life
Objectives	$	$3,750	$3,750	$2,500	$1,500
S.S. and/or Other Govt. Benefits		1,072	536	—	892
Continuing Income (Husband)		2,500	2500	2500	245
Present Requirements	$	$178	$714	$ —	$363

Capital Amounts: $ — / 16,900 / 30,600 / — / 28,600 / $76,100

TOTAL PRESENT REQUIREMENTS

If __Bill__ Dies $183,645 (Husband)   If __Nancy__ Dies $138,845 (Wife)

Side 1

ILL. 5.15 ■ Total Needs Work Sheet (side 2)

PRESENT REQUIREMENTS vs. PRESENT RESOURCES

If _Bill_ Dies   If _Nancy_ Dies
     (Husband)   (Wife)

	If Bill Dies	If Nancy Dies
Total Present Capital Requirements	$183,645	$138,845
Present Life Insurance Applicable	$36,600	$28,600
Other Present Asset Values Applicable	$8,000	$8,000
Total Present Capital Resources	$44,600	$36,600
New Life Insurance Required	$139,045	$102,245

NEW INSURANCE RECOMMENDED

On _Bill_ $139,000 $50,000 WL + $89,000 10-yr. Term $103 / mo
   (Husband)   (Amount)   (Policy or Combination of Policies)   (Premium)

On _Nancy_ $102,000 $30,000 WL + $72,000 10-yr. Term $47 / mo
   (Wife)   (Amount)   (Policy or Combination of Policies)   (Premium)

LIVING VALUES

RETIREMENT INCOME

For _Bill_ at _65_ AND _Nancy_ at _65_ – _20_
   (Husband)   (age)   (Wife)   (age)   (year)

From:

		Option or Earnings Rate	Monthly Life Income
Social Security and/or Other Gov't Benefits	Bill (Husband)		$892
	Nancy (Wife)		676
Pension and/or Profit Sharing Plans	Bill (Husband)		245
	Nancy (Wife)		195
Present Life Insurance	Bill (Husband)	(20-yr. cert.)	14 *
	Nancy (Wife)	(20-yr. cert.)	7 *
New Life Insurance	Bill (Husband)	(20-yr. cert.)	114 *
	Nancy (Wife)	(20-yr. cert.)	60 *
Other			

* See Ill. 5.18.

Total Monthly Retirement Income $2,203

MISCELLANEOUS (Education, Opportunity, Emergency Funds, etc.)

If needed for education purposes, there would be approximately:

— $17,200 at Susan's age 18 or

— $23,000 at Tad's age 18 or

— $11,500 at Susan's age 18 and $11,500 at Tad's age 18

(Any of these values must be repaid or replaced, of course, if retirement values are to stand.)

Side 2

improves, Bill and Nancy will be able to convert all or part of the level term to whole life. The added whole life will build additional cash surrender values for retirement income.

Finally, the plan satisfies the objectives for both spouses in the two-income situation if one dies. Both are treated in an equitable manner; both need additional life insurance to satisfy their own objectives.

▪ SALES KIT

For the sales kit, we'll look only at the "Family Financial Summary" (Ill. 5.16) and the "Recommendations and Key Benefits" sheet (Ill. 5.17). The other items are the same as in the study that we covered earlier.

We have seen how practical application of the capital utilization method can satisfy total needs in both one-income and two-income family situations. In either case, they get the job done—and in a way that is interesting, understandable and appealing to the prospective buyers.

The "Family Financial Summary" does an equally good job of presenting the two-income and the one-income family cases. It is becoming popular, especially with large, complex cases, because it includes all items for both spouses—even the small need or no-need items.

The outline summary also works particularly well with the capital retention methods discussed in the next chapter. In the outline form the amounts of new life insurance required to satisfy objectives are clearly established. Whichever is used, the "Recommendations and Key Benefits" sheet is needed to complete the presentation, so let's examine it.

The only item not picked up from the work sheet is the paid-up insurance available at retirement age. The explanation is simple.

Some of the cash value—about $750 per $1,000 face amount at age 65 or $745 per $1,000 at age 62—may be used to provide paid-up insurance rather than retirement income. These amounts would only provide a little under $4 of life income 20-year certain. Thus, Bill and Nancy may have paid-up insurance when they retire at an exchange rate of about $1,000 paid-up insurance for each $4 deducted from the monthly retirement income.

ILL. 5.16 ■ Family Financial Summary

PREPARED FOR: *Bill and Nancy*　　　　　　　　DATE: *1/8*

FAMILY FINANCIAL SUMMARY

	For *Nancy* (Wife) if *Bill* (Husband) should die.	For *Bill* (Husband) if *Nancy* (Wife) should die.
CASH NEEDS		
Final Expenses — Objective	$ *11,000*	$ *11,000*
Less Social Security and/or Other Govt. Benefits	$ *255*	$ *255*
Present Requirement	$ *10,745*	$ *10,745*
Your Housing Fund — Present Requirement	$ *18,000*	$ *12,000*
Your Children's Education — Objective	$ *40,000*	$ *40,000*
Less Social Security and/or Other Govt. Benefits	$ *—*	$ *—*
Present Requirement	$ *40,000*	$ *40,000*
Total Cash Needs	$ *68,745*	$ *62,745*
MONTHLY INCOME NEEDS		
Dependency Period — 3 or more eligible — Objective	$ *3,500*	$ *—*
Less Social Security and/or Other Govt. Benefits	$ *1,637*	$ *—*
Less Continuing Personal Income	$ *1,667*	$ *—*
Present Requirement (Income–Capital)	$ *196* – $ *18,600*	$ *—* – $ *—*
Dependency Period — 2 eligible — Objective	$ *3,500*	$ *3,750*
Less Social Security and/or Other Govt. Benefits	$ *917*	$ *1,072*
Less Continuing Personal Income	$ *1,667*	$ *2,500*
Present Requirement (Income–Capital)	$ *916* – $ *24,200*	$ *178* – $ *16,900*
Dependency Period — 1 eligible — Objective	$ *3,000*	$ *3,750*
Less Social Security and/or Other Govt. Benefits	$ *720*	$ *536*
Less Continuing Personal Income	$ *1,667*	$ *2,500*
Present Requirement (Income–Capital)	$ *613* – $ *10,100*	$ *714* – $ *30,600*
For spouse (no children) — Objective	$ *2,000*	$ *2,500*
— to Age	*65*	*65*
Less Continuing Personal Income	$ *1,667*	$ *2,500*
Present Requirement (Income–Capital)	$ *333* – $ *33,700*	$ *—* – $ *—*
For spouse (no children) — Objective	$ *1,500*	$ *1,500*
— for Life After Age	*65*	*65*
Less Social Security and/or Other Govt. Benefits	$ *961*	$ *892*
Less Continuing Personal Income	$ *195*	$ *245*
Present Requirement (Income–Capital)	$ *344* – $ *28,300*	$ *363* – $ *28,600*
Total Capital to Satisfy Income Needs	$ *114,900*	$ *76,100*
Total Capital to Satisfy Cash and Income Needs	$ *183,645*	$ *138,845*
Less Existing Life Insurance and Other Assets	$ *44,600*	$ *36,600*
Amount Still Required to Satisfy Your Objectives	$ *139,045*	$ *102,245*

RECOMMENDATIONS:

New Life Insurance of:

$139,000 on Bill — $50,000 WL with WP and $89,000 10-yr. term $103/mo

$102,000 on Nancy — $30,000 WL with WP and $72,000 10-yr. term $47/mo

$150/mo

RETIREMENT INCOME if you live, starting at *Bill* (Husband) 's age *65* and *Nancy* (Wife) 's age *65* :

From Social Security and/or Other Government Benefit Plans	$ *1,568*
From Present Insurance, Employee Retirement Plans and Other Resources	$ *461*
From Recommended New Life Insurance	$ *174*
Total Retirement Income	$ *2,203*

ILL. 5.17 ■ Recommendations and Key Benefits

A. POLICY RECOMMENDATIONS

To provide the additional capital required to satisfy your family financial objectives completely if either of you should not live, it is recommended that you purchase additional life insurance as follows:

On Bill's life—

$50,000 Whole Life with Disability Waiver of Premium and $89,000 Ten-Year Convertible Level Term	Monthly Premium	$103

On Nancy's life—

$30,000 Whole Life with Disability Waiver of Premium and $72,000 Ten-Year Convertible Level Term	Monthly Premium	$ 47
	Total New Monthly Premium	$150

B. RETIREMENT INCOME

If the recommended program is adopted, your combined monthly retirement income at Bill's age 65 and Nancy's age 65 will be as follows:

From Social Security—	Bill's own	$892	
	Nancy's own	676	$1,568
From pension and present insurance*	Bill	$259	
	Nancy	202	$ 461
From new life insurance*	Bill	$114	
	Nancy	60	$ 174
Total combined monthly retirement income			$2,203

*If desired a few thousand dollars of the life insurance may be set aside for a continuing Final Expense Fund. The retirement income will be reduced by only about $4 per month for each $1,000 set aside as paid-up insurance on Bill and Nancy.

C. EDUCATION FUNDS

Under this plan substantial funds clearly have been provided for the education of Susan and Tad if either of you should die. But what if you both live? In that event, the recommended program will make education funds available as follows:

	At Susan's Age 18		At Tad's Age 18
From loans on present insurance†	$ 2,100	OR	$ 2,400
From loans on new insurance†	7,100	OR	12,600
From other liquid assets (estimate)	8,000	OR	8,000
Total funds available	17,200	OR	23,000
OR—by dividing the funds equally	$11,500	AND	$11,500

†Any insurance loan values used for educational purposes must be repaid or replaced, of course, if the above retirement income is to be available.

ILL. 5.18 ■ Interest Option or Earnings (Sample Table)

Monthly Income From Each $1,000 at Various Rates of Interest (Payments at End of Month)

%	$	%	$
1½	1.24	5¼	4.27
1¾	1.45	5½	4.47
		5¾	4.67
2	1.65	6	4.87
2¼	1.86	6¼	5.06
2½	2.06	6½	5.26
2¾	2.26	6¾	5.46
3	2.47	7	5.65
3¼	2.67	7½	6.04
3½	2.87		
3¾	3.07	8	6.43
		8½	6.82
4	3.27		
4¼	3.47	9	7.21
4½	3.67	9½	7.59
4¾	3.87		
5	4.07	10	7.97

■ CHAPTER 5 QUESTIONS FOR REVIEW

1. How much money will it take to provide an income of $500 a month for three years at 3 percent? (See Ill. 5.19.)

   a. $17,250
   b. $5,590
   c. $80,378
   d. $69,810

2. The present value of $1 five years from now, assuming 5 percent interest, is:

   a. .7835.
   b. .8219.
   c. .6139.
   d. .8626.

3. What needs make up the total present requirements?

   a. Total cash needs and total monthly needs
   b. Total monthly needs and life insurance needs
   c. Total cash needs and total capital needs
   d. Final monthly needs and present insurance total

ILL. 5.19 ■ Fixed Period (Amount) Option Table

Amounts Required To Provide Various Monthly Incomes
3%

Years of Income	$10	$20	$25	$50	$75	$100	$125	$150
1	$ 119	$ 237	$ 296	$ 592	$ 888	$ 1,184	$ 1,480	$ 1,776
2	234	467	583	1,167	1,750	2,333	2,916	3,500
3	345	690	862	1,725	2,587	3,449	4,311	5,174
4	454	907	1,133	2,267	3,400	4,533	5,667	6,800
5	559	1,117	1,396	2,793	4,189	5,585	6,981	8,378
6	661	1,321	1,652	3,303	4,955	6,606	8,258	9,909
7	760	1,520	1,899	3,799	5,698	7,597	9,496	11,396
8	856	1,712	2,140	4,280	6,420	8,560	10,700	12,840
9	950	1,899	2,374	4,747	7,121	9,494	11,868	14,241
10	1,040	2,081	2,601	5,201	7,802	10,402	13,003	15,603
11	1,128	2,257	2,821	5,642	8,462	11,283	14,104	16,925
12	1,214	2,428	3,035	6,069	9,104	12,138	15,173	18,207
13	1,297	2,594	3,242	6,484	9,726	12,968	16,210	19,452
14	1,378	2,755	3,444	6,888	10,331	13,775	17,219	20,663
15	1,456	2,912	3,639	7,279	10,918	14,557	18,196	21,836
16	1,532	3,064	3,829	7,659	11,488	15,317	19,146	22,976
17	1,606	3,211	4,014	8,028	12,041	16,055	20,069	24,083
18	1,677	3,354	4,193	8,386	12,578	16,771	20,964	25,157
19	1,747	3,494	4,367	8,734	13,100	17,467	21,834	26,201
20	1,814	3,629	4,536	9,071	13,607	18,142	22,678	27,213
21	1,880	3,760	4,699	9,399	14,098	18,797	23,496	28,196
22	1,944	3,887	4,859	9,717	14,576	19,434	24,293	29,151
23	2,005	4,010	5,013	10,026	15,039	20,052	25,065	30,078
24	2,065	4,130	5,163	10,326	15,488	20,651	25,814	30,977
25	2,124	4,247	5,309	10,617	15,926	21,234	26,543	31,851
26	2,180	4,360	5,450	10,900	16,349	21,799	27,249	32,699
27	2,235	4,470	5,587	11,174	16,761	22,348	27,935	33,522
28	2,288	4,576	5,720	11,441	17,161	22,881	28,601	34,322
29	2,340	4,680	5,850	11,700	17,549	23,399	29,249	35,099
30	2,390	4,780	5,975	11,951	17,926	23,901	29,876	35,852

ILL. 5.20 ■ Present Value (Discount) Table

Deposit Required Now at Various Rates of Compound Interest to Equal $1 at the End of a Designated Number of Years

Years	3%	3½%	4%	4½%	5%	5½%	6%	6½%	7%	8%	9%	10%
1	$.9709	$.9662	$.9615	$.9569	$.9524	$.9479	$.9434	$.939	$.935	$.926	$.917	$.909
2	.9426	.9335	.9246	.9157	.9070	.8985	.8900	.882	.873	.857	.842	.826
3	.9151	.9019	.8890	.8763	.8638	.8516	.8396	.828	.816	.794	.772	.751
4	.8885	.8714	.8548	.8386	.8227	.8072	.7921	.777	.763	.735	.708	.683
5	.8626	.8420	.8219	.8025	.7835	.7651	.7473	.730	.713	.681	.650	.621
6	.8375	.8135	.7903	.7679	.7462	.7252	.7050	.685	.666	.630	.596	.564
7	.8131	.7860	.7599	.7348	.7107	.6874	.6651	.644	.623	.583	.547	.513
8	.7894	.7594	.7307	.7032	.6768	.6516	.6274	.604	.582	.540	.502	.467
9	.7664	.7337	.7026	.6729	.6446	.6176	.5919	.567	.544	.500	.460	.424
10	.7441	.7089	.6756	.6439	.6139	.5854	.5584	.533	.508	.463	.422	.386
11	.7224	.6849	.6496	.6162	.5847	.5549	.5268	.500	.475	.429	.388	.350
12	.7014	.6618	.6246	.5897	.5568	.5260	.4970	.470	.444	.397	.356	.319
13	.6810	.6394	.6006	.5643	.5303	.4986	.4688	.441	.415	.368	.326	.290
14	.6611	.6178	.5775	.5400	.5051	.4726	.4423	.414	.388	.340	.299	.263
15	.6419	.5969	.5553	.5167	.4810	.4479	.4173	.389	.362	.315	.275	.239
16	.6232	.5767	.5339	.4945	.4581	.4246	.3936	.365	.339	.292	.252	.218
17	.6050	.5572	.5134	.4732	.4363	.4024	.3714	.343	.317	.270	.231	.198
18	.5874	.5384	.4936	.4528	.4155	.3815	.3503	.322	.296	.250	.212	.180
19	.5703	.5202	.4746	.4333	.3957	.3616	.3305	.302	.277	.232	.194	.164
20	.5537	.5026	.4564	.4146	.3769	.3427	.3118	.284	.258	.215	.178	.149
21	.5375	.4856	.4388	.3968	.3589	.3249	.2942	.266	.242	.199	.164	.135
22	.5219	.4692	.4220	.3797	.3418	.3079	.2775	.250	.226	.189	.150	.123
23	.5067	.4533	.4057	.3634	.3256	.2919	.2618	.235	.211	.170	.138	.112
24	.4919	.4380	.3901	.3477	.3101	.2767	.2470	.221	.197	.158	.126	.102
25	.4776	.4231	.3751	.3327	.2953	.2622	.2330	.207	.184	.146	.116	.092
26	.4637	.4088	.3607	.3184	.2812	.2486	.2198	.194	.172	.135	.106	.084
27	.4502	.3950	.3468	.3047	.2678	.2356	.2074	.183	.161	.125	.098	.076
28	.4371	.3817	.3335	.2916	.2551	.2233	.1956	.171	.150	.116	.090	.069
29	.4243	.3687	.3207	.2790	.2429	.2117	.1846	.161	.141	.107	.082	.063
30	.4120	.3563	.3083	.2670	.2314	.2006	.1741	.151	.131	.099	.075	.057
31	.4000	.3442	.2965	.2555	.2204	.1902	.1643	.142	.123	.092	.069	.052
32	.3883	.3326	.2851	.2445	.2099	.1803	.1550	.133	.115	.085	.063	.047
33	.3770	.3213	.2741	.2340	.1999	.1709	.1462	.125	.107	.079	.058	.043
34	.3660	.3105	.2636	.2239	.1904	.1620	.1379	.118	.100	.073	.053	.039
35	.3554	.3000	.2534	.2143	.1813	.1535	.1301	.110	.094	.068	.049	.036
36	.3450	.2898	.2437	.2050	.1727	.1455	.1227	.104	.088	.063	.045	.032
37	.3350	.2800	.2343	.1962	.1644	.1379	.1158	.097	.082	.058	.041	.029
38	.3252	.2706	.2253	.1878	.1566	.1307	.1092	.091	.076	.054	.038	.027
39	.3158	.2614	.2166	.1797	.1491	.1239	.1031	.086	.071	.050	.035	.024
40	.3066	.2526	.2083	.1719	.1420	.1175	.0972	.081	.067	.046	.032	.022
41	.2976	.2440	.2003	.1645	.1353	.1113	.0917	.076	.062	.043	.029	.020
42	.2890	.2358	.1926	.1574	.1288	.1055	.0865	.071	.058	.039	.027	.018
43	.2805	.2278	.1852	.1507	.1227	.1000	.0816	.067	.055	.037	.025	.017
44	.2724	.2201	.1780	.1442	.1169	.0948	.0770	.063	.051	.034	.023	.015
45	.2644	.2127	.1712	.1380	.1113	.0899	.0726	.059	.048	.031	.021	.014
46	.2567	.2055	.1646	.1320	.1060	.0852	.0685	.055	.044	.029	.019	.012
47	.2493	.1985	.1583	.1263	.1009	.0807	.0647	.052	.042	.027	.017	.011
48	.2420	.1918	.1522	.1209	.0961	.0765	.0610	.049	.039	.025	.016	.010
49	.2350	.1853	.1463	.1157	.0916	.0725	.0575	.046	.036	.023	.015	.009
50	.2281	.1791	.1407	.1107	.0872	.0688	.0543	.043	.034	.021	.013	.009

ILL. 5.21 ■ Life Income Option Table

Amounts Required to Provide $10 Monthly Life Income at Various Ages

(1937 Standard Annuity Table — Rated Down One Year)

3%

Male Age	Female Age	Life Income Only	5 Years Certain and Life	10 Years Certain and Life	15 Years Certain and Life	20 Years Certain and Life
15	20	$3,205	$3,205	$3,205	$3,215	$3,226
20	25	3,086	3,086	3,096	3,096	3,115
25	30	2,950	2,950	2,958	2,976	2,985
30	35	2,801	2,801	2,801	2,825	2,849
31	36	2,770	2,770	2,778	2,793	2,825
32	37	2,732	2,740	2,747	2,762	2,793
33	38	2,703	2,703	2,717	2,732	2,762
34	39	2,667	2,667	2,681	2,703	2,732
35	40	2,632	2,632	2,646	2,667	2,703
36	41	2,597	2,597	2,611	2,639	2,674
37	42	2,558	2,564	2,577	2,604	2,646
38	43	2,519	2,525	2,545	2,571	2,611
39	44	2,488	2,488	2,506	2,538	2,584
40	45	2,445	2,451	2,469	2,500	2,551
41	46	2,410	2,415	2,433	2,469	2,519
42	47	2,375	2,375	2,398	2,433	2,488
43	48	2,331	2,336	2,358	2,398	2,457
44	49	2,288	2,299	2,320	2,364	2,427
45	50	2,247	2,257	2,283	2,331	2,398
46	51	2,208	2,217	2,247	2,294	2,364
47	52	2,165	2,174	2,208	2,257	2,336
48	53	2,123	2,132	2,169	2,222	2,304
49	54	2,079	2,092	2,128	2,188	2,278
50	55	2,037	2,049	2,088	2,155	2,247
51	56	2,008	2,008	2,049	2,119	2,222
52	57	1,953	1,965	2,012	2,088	2,193
53	58	1,908	1,908	1,972	2,053	2,165
54	59	1,862	1,880	1,931	2,020	2,137
55	60	1,818	1,838	1,894	1,984	2,114
56	61	1,776	1,795	1,855	1,953	2,088
57	62	1,730	1,751	1,815	1,919	2,066
58	63	1,686	1,709	1,776	1,890	2,041
59	64	1,642	1,667	1,739	1,859	2,020
60	65	1,597	1,623	1,701	1,828	2,000
61	66	1,553	1,580	1,664	1,802	1,980
62	67	1,508	1,538	1,629	1,773	1,961
63	68	1,464	1,495	1,592	1,745	1,946
64	69	1,418	1,453	1,560	1,721	1,927
65	70	1,376	1,412	1,522	1,695	1,912
70	75	1,160	1,214	1,366	1,590	1,859
75	80	958	1,034	1,238	1,520	1,828

4. The basis for most computer methods is:

    a. present value.
    b. interest only.
    c. compounded income.
    d. interest lay-back.

5. The first *Present Requirement* is:

    a. converted to capital needed and discounted two years.
    b. converted to capital needed and entered as the first capital amount.
    c. discounted at the proper time, then converted to capital needed.
    d. None of the above

6

Capital Retention Method

T his chapter will explain the capital retention method of total needs selling and why it is so popular. You will learn when to use this method and how to use it. The steps in the sale will be analyzed to show how the procedures differ from the capital utilization method. You'll learn the difference between the simple method and the present value or discount methods of determining present requirements.

■ ■ ■ ■ ■

The very popular capital retention approach to the total needs method of life insurance selling is described in this chapter. Techniques comprising capital retention methods are widely used as a result of the efforts of proponents such as Tom Wolff and his "Capital Need Analysis." The main characteristic of capital retention methods is that only the *earnings* on invested capital are used to satisfy income requirements. The capital itself—unlike in the capital utilization method—is not used for income payments.

Before focusing on the variations, the mechanics and the results of capital retention, let's consider why it is now a possible alternative for many people.

■ WHY CAPITAL RETENTION?

There are three main reasons for the rise in popularity of the capital retention method:

1. Social Security benefits and employee benefit plans now provide a substantial portion of a prospect's survivorship income needs.
2. Interest yields on invested capital have increased greatly in recent years.
3. Many middle-income families enjoy substantial incomes that make large amounts of life insurance affordable.

Appeals to Prospects

Capital retention appeals to prospects because:

1. The idea of creating sufficient capital, living on the earnings, then passing the capital to children or other heirs is very appealing to most people.
2. The concepts are easy to understand—even the language normally is more familiar to prospects than the terminology pertaining to settlement options.
3. The approach is refreshingly new and different to many prospects.
4. With this method, providing a hedge against inflation is considerably easier than with the use of settlement options.
5. Although relatively simple, capital retention methods suggest an aura of financial sophistication generally reserved for the well-to-do and thus offer a trace of ego satisfaction for many prospects.
6. Capital retention methods permit maximum flexibility—decisions can be delayed until the actual needs arise.

Appeals to Life Insurance Agents

Capital retention appeals to life insurance agents because:

1. The great appeal to prospects represents a noteworthy advantage to agents.
2. Planning and presentation steps are considerably easier than with other methods and require less paperwork, calculations and explanations.
3. Service is easier and less time-consuming.
4. It appeals to higher income and more sophisticated prospects.
5. Needs for capital are greater, so sales are larger.
6. It is readily adaptable to one-income or two-income families.
7. It provides an appealing, modern means of selling life insurance on a total needs basis to satisfy the agent's responsibilities to prospects and clients.

Although capital retention appeals to many people, it is not appropriate for everyone. In fact, the capital utilization method generally is used instead of capital retention for people of quite modest means, for situations requiring both capital and earnings to satisfy objectives or for situations requiring the fixed-dollar guarantees of settlement options. You must use good judgment to determine which system best fits a particular prospect. The characteristics of a good prospect for the capital retention method are discussed later.

■ HISTORY OF THE CONCEPT

The basic concept underlying capital retention originated more than 100 years ago as the only means of solving income need problems before the understanding and use of settlement options became common among life insurance agents during the Depression. It has remained popular ever since. This concept simply is to create a capital fund of sufficient size to:

1. satisfy all *cash* needs from the capital;
2. satisfy all *income* needs from earnings on the remaining capital and
3. pass the *capital* on intact to the heirs when there is no longer a need for income.

Using just earnings to provide income is the only real difference between the capital retention and capital utilization methods. It's that difference, with the obvious advantage of preserving capital for children or other heirs, that makes capital retention a good idea today for the right people under the right circumstances.

Several popular total needs selling methods are based on the concept of conserving capital. These methods are called by various names: Capital Analysis, Capital Retention, Capital Need Analysis, etc. Actually, although some of these methods may be more complex than others, all are basically the same. So we'll discuss all of them under the descriptive title of "Capital Retention Methods."

■ WHEN TO USE CAPITAL RETENTION METHODS

Capital retention methods are designed to help families whose income producers die too soon or live too long. Obviously, then, the prospects should be part of either a one-income or two-income family situation and have a sincere interest in the well-being of the other family members. Because capital retention methods may call for more capital than previously discussed methods, they often require larger amounts of new insurance. So the best prospects for capital retention methods generally earn above-average incomes.

Ideally, prospects should own significant amounts of life insurance and a reasonable amount of other investable assets. However, because the need for new insurance will equal the deficit between capital requirements and capital resources, the best prospects generally are not the *very* wealthy, in terms of present capital resources.

In summary, the best prospects for capital retention methods are members of one-income or two-income families with:

1. relatively high current incomes;
2. reasonable amounts of current insurance and wealth and
3. children or others to whom they want to leave substantial amounts of capital when their needs and/or their spouses' needs end.

■ STEPS IN THE SALE

Many of the steps in the capital utilization sale apply to capital retention methods. We won't repeat these steps here. Follow the same general procedures in the capital retention sale—fact-finding, engineering the plan and wrapping up the sale—that you do when using capital utilization methods. The steps virtually are identical in all phases except "engineering the plan," where you calculate the amount of insurance required to do the job. Let's concentrate on that specific phase in this discussion of capital retention methods.

Determining Capital Requirements

The steps involved in determining the amounts needed to satisfy *cash* needs are identical to those used in Chapter 5. However, the *income* needs are determined differently, because we're concerned with providing the needed income only from *capital earnings*. Liquidation of capital through the use of settlement options is not involved.

Inflation has existed for a long time and probably will continue, at least at some rate. This has created concern about the viability of long-range financial plans based on today's dollars. Capital retention provides a measure of protection against inflation. If the inflationary trend continues, interest earnings on retained capital most likely will increase at approximately the same rate as the inflation rate. In addition, the fact that a nondepleting capital account is available means that there will be a resource to dip into if, over brief periods, earnings fall short of the income needed.

However, dipping into capital reduces the capital fund for creating interest or investment earnings. It also may deplete the capital before the need for it ends. To combat this, many life insurance agents are turning to innovative ways to build inflation protection into their proposed plans. One method builds an "inflation factor" into the present requirements phase of calculating the amount of new insurance needed. While the specifics of various methods vary, they all include a preselected assumed annual rate of inflation over the period of years that income will be needed.

For example, an agent and client may decide together that they should plan for an annual inflation rate of 4 percent over the next 20 years. Using present value tables similar to those used in Chapter 5, they determine that the capital required over the full 20-year period will be substantially greater than if inflation were not a factor. If the plan is to do the job it is designed to do, that larger amount will be needed.

This "inflated" amount can look like an insurmountable figure to someone who is thinking in terms of today's dollar, today's economy; that's where the real selling effort takes place. It may be necessary to work with your prospects on increasing the amount they originally had indicated in the fact-finding form to put into a plan; you may need to review the various needs to determine where adjustments can be made.

In essence, the task of determining the capital required to produce desired income entails converting the monthly income requirements into present requirements. In the case of capital retention, these are the amounts sufficient to generate monthly interest earnings equal to the income requirements. Two ways of performing the conversion are (1) the simple method and (2) the present value or discount method.

The Simple Method

This method condenses everything down to just about one task. From your work sheet, you determine the period during which the largest monthly income need will arise; then do a quick mathematical calculation to arrive at the total *Capital Amount* that—at whatever rate of interest or investment return you use—will yield earnings equal to that income. If that amount is enough to yield earnings equal to the largest monthly income needed in the highest income need period, it's going to be more than enough to do the job in the other periods.

An illustration of the *Monthly Income Needs* section of the work sheet is shown as Ill. 6.1. As in the capital utilization chapters, we've marked the columns A, B, C, D and E for easy reference.

Here are the procedures:

1. Look across the *Present Requirements* row and select the highest monthly income amount required in any period (Column D in the example).

ILL. 6.1 ▪ Simple Method

	A	B	C	D	E
	For____ Depend. Yrs While 3 or More Elig	For____ Depend. Yrs While 2 Eligible	For____ Depend. Yrs While 1 Eligible	For_____ Yrs. Until Wife is Age _____	Wife for Life
Objectives	$	$	$	$	$
S. S. and/or Other Govt. Benefits					
Continuing Income (Wife)					
Present Requirements	$ *800*	$ *950*	$ *1,200*	$ *1,500*	$ *1,200*
Capital Amounts $_____					
_____					
300,000					
$ *300,000*	$ *800*	$ *950*	$ *1,200*	$ *1,500*	$ *1,200*

2. Now the mathematical exercise begins. Your task is to determine the full capital amount—at an assumed rate of interest—that will yield earnings equal to that income need. To achieve this, divide the largest income need by the assumed interest rate. Because we're looking at monthly earnings, it's necessary to use the approximate monthly equivalent of the annual assumed earnings. Your answer is then entered on the top and bottom lines on the far left side of the page, in the *Capital Amounts* box.

For example, after fact-finding, you determine that your clients are good prospects for capital retention. Using the simple method, follow these steps:

- First, all of you agree that 6 percent annual interest is a reasonable figure to yield earnings equal to the client's income needs of $1,500.
- Second, to determine the *monthly* interest based on the 6 percent *annual* interest, divide 6 percent by twelve months ($.06 \div 12 = .005$).
- Third, use that number, .005, to calculate the capital amount required to create $1,500 monthly income. That's $1,500 \div .005 = $300,000. This means that, at 6 percent a year, $300,000 will provide $1,500 per month. Enter $300,000 in the *Capital Amounts* box in Ill. 6.1.

When the highest income need period has been satisfied, any surplus capital no longer required to satisfy subsequent income needs may be passed on to children or other heirs early as gifts. This is one reason for using the capital retention method. The same procedures usually must be followed for the other spouse.

The Present Value or Discount Method

Generally, the present value or discount method more closely approximates the capital amount needed (usually a lesser amount) because it avoids income in excess of needs in some of the income periods. It does this by compounding earnings through lower income need periods to increase the capital available during any subsequent higher income need periods.

Let's walk through the present value or discount method of capital retention planning. Our example is keyed to Ill. 6.2.

First, the monthly amounts needed are determined just as they are in the capital utilization method. The income objectives for each income period are listed on the work sheet. The Social Security benefits that are available and any continuing income are subtracted from that target income amount to find the monthly income needed.

The system differs when determining the *Capital Amounts*. Since only the earnings on invested capital are used to satisfy income requirements, the capital is preserved. Let's assume that the monthly income needed in the first income period is $800, and the interest rate is 6 percent. First, divide $800 by assumed monthly net earnings: $800 ÷ .005 = $160,000. This is the first capital amount and should be entered on the first line of the *Capital Amounts* box.

Now go to the second income period and find the monthly income needed. Let's assume that it's $950. Note that $800 of this needed income is already being provided by the capital from the first income period. Subtract the second needed income from the first ($950 − $800). Write $800 on the line below $950 and write the difference on the line below that. In this case it is $150. Divide *this* amount, $150, by the assumed monthly net earnings: $150 ÷ .005 = $30,000. Since this amount isn't needed immediately, it should be discounted to it's present value determined by using Ill. 5.20. Let's assume a five-year period before the amount in the second income period is needed. The amount obtained is the capital amount for the second income period: .7473 × $30,000 = $22,419 ($22,400 rounded down). Write that amount on the second line in the *Capital Amounts* box.

Let's say that the monthly income needed for the third income period is $1,200. Again, note that $950 of that income is being earned by the capital already provided in the first and second income periods. Capital is needed for an additional $250 ($1,200 − $950 = $250). Divide this amount by the assumed monthly net earnings: $250 ÷ .005 = $50,000. This amount also must be discounted to its present value since it is not needed immediately. Let's assume a four-year period before the

ILL. 6.2 ■ Present Value or Discount Method

Present Requirements	$ A	$ B	$ C	$ D	$ E
	$ 800	$ 950	$ 1,200	$ 1,500	$ 1,200
Capital Amounts—					
$ 160,000	$ 800	$ 800	$ 800	$ 800	$ 800
22,400		150	150	150	150
29,600			250	250	250
29,800				300	300
—					—
$ 241,800	$ 800	$ 950	$ 1,200	$ 1,500	$ 1,500

ILL. 6.3 ■ Capital Retention Step-by-Step Procedures

CAPITAL RETENTION
The Present Value or Discount Method

Step 1. Determine cash needs from fact-finding.

    a. Objectives:
        Final Expenses
        Housing Fund
        Education Fund
          minus
    b. Social Security and/or Other Govt. Benefits
          equals
    c. Present Requirements, for money to meet cash needs at death

Step 2. Identify the different income need periods, based on the surviving spouse's age and number of dependent children.

    a. First Income Period—starts at the surviving spouse's present age and is defined by the number of dependents still at home. If there are two or more children below age 16, use the first column (*While three or more eligible*); if there is only one child at home, use the next column (*While two eligible*), etc.
    b. Second Income Period—starts when first child no longer receives Social Security benefits; only surviving spouse and remaining child(ren) receive benefits.
    c. Third Income Period—starts when youngest child turns 16.
    d. Fourth Income Period—starts when youngest (and last eligible) child turns 18; this begins the blackout period for the surviving spouse.
    e. Fifth Income Period—starts at the surviving spouse's retirement.

Step 3. Determine income needs for each income period, using fact-finding form and *Guide to Social Security*.

    a. Objectives (the income needed for each income period)
          minus
    b. Social Security and/or Other Govt. Benefits payable during each income period
          minus
    c. Continuing Income to be received during each income period
          equals
    d. Present Requirements, the additional monthly income needed to meet that period's objectives

Step 4. Convert the Present Requirement income needs into Capital Amounts that will produce this income for each period.

    a. First Income Period—divide the first period income need by the assumed monthly net earnings.

    Example: Assume $500 is needed monthly and annual interest rate is 6 percent:

$$.06 \div 12 \text{ months} = .005 \text{ per month}$$
$$\$500 \div .005 = \$100,000$$

    $100,000 is the capital amount necessary for the first income period. Since this period begins immediately, this amount *is not discounted.* Enter this amount on the first line in the *Capital Amounts* box.

    b. Remaining Income Periods—determine the additional income need by subtracting the previous income amounts from all previous income periods (these amounts have been capitalized and are producing income).

ILL. 6.3 ■ Capital Retention Step-by-Step Procedures (continued)

Divide the remaining income needed by the assumed monthly net earnings and discount it for the proper time, by using the present value of $1, in Ill. 5.20.

Example: Assume $800 is needed monthly in the second income period. The first period, with an income need of $500, lasted eight years:

$800 – $500 = $300 additional needed per month for
second income period

$300 ÷ .005 = $60,000 Capital Amount

This $60,000 will not be needed for eight years, so it is discounted. The present value of $1 for eight years at 6 percent is .6274:

$60,000 × .6274 = $37,644 ($37,600 rounded)

These amounts should be entered on the second and following lines in the *Capital Amounts* box.

Step 5. Determine *all* cash and income (capital) needs.

  a. Total Cash Needs for final expenses, housing fund and education fund
    plus
  b. Capital Amounts from all income periods
    equals
  c. Total Present Requirements

Step 6. Determine present deficit.

  a. Total Present Requirements
    minus
  b. Present Life Insurance
    minus
  c. Other Present Asset Values
    equals
  d. NEW LIFE INSURANCE NEEDED

amount in the third income period is needed. Add the five years from the first to the second income period, and the four years from the second to the third income period to get nine years before this income is needed. In nine years, $50,000 discounted to present value at 6 percent is .5919 × $50,000 = $29,595 ($29,600 rounded). Write the rounded amount on the third line in the *Capital Amounts* box.

In the fourth income period, the monthly amount needed is $1,500. Once more, we see that $1,200 of this income is provided by accumulated capital. Capital is needed for an additional $300 ($1,500 – $1,200 = $300). Divide this amount by the assumed monthly net earnings: $300 ÷ .005 = $60,000. This amount also must be discounted to its present value since it is not needed immediately. Let's assume a three-year period before the amount in the fourth income period is needed. Following the procedure described in the third period above, add the years before this income is needed: 5 + 4 + 3 = 12 years. In twelve years, $60,000 discounted to present value at 6 percent is .4970 × $60,000 = $29,820 ($29,800 rounded). Write that amount on the fourth line in the *Capital Amounts* box.

In the *For Life* column, we find that the monthly amount needed is $1,200. Since capital for a monthly income of $1,500 has been accumulated by this time, no additional capital is required (see Ill. 6.2).

Repeat these procedures for the lower half of the work sheet if there are income needs in the event of the other spouse's death.

Incidentally, this capital retention method should be used only when the prospect's present general assets equal or exceed the present value of any capital on which earnings are to be held until the start of a future income period. The reason, of course, is that the only capital that can grow from now until some future time is capital that exists now. Life insurance proceeds will not be available for such compounding until after the insured's death.

This is not a problem in the present value *capital utilization* method. In that case, if the insured dies immediately, the life insurance proceeds will be there immediately for compounding. If the insured dies later, the excess insurance proceeds—that is, the proceeds no longer needed to provide income between now and the time of death—will be available to offset the earlier lack of compounding.

In *capital retention*, however, no proceeds are to be used to provide income at any time—*only earnings* are used. Thus, there are no excess proceeds to offset any lack of compounding prior to the insured's death. Unless present general assets are adequate to cover present values to be held from now until a future income need period, there might not be enough capital to provide all of the earnings needed in that period.

Use this present value or discount method only when enough present general assets are available to avoid this problem. Otherwise, the "simple" method described earlier is better. It may produce more earnings than needed during some periods, but it's much safer.

Calculating New Insurance Amounts

The method of calculating new insurance amounts is practically identical for the capital retention and the capital utilization methods. Just subtract present assets from total present capital requirements. The answer represents the new life insurance required to satisfy total income and cash needs if one or both spouses die.

This is where some agents plug in the inflation factor discussed earlier in this chapter. The amount arrived at by this exercise represents the amount that will be needed, assuming the dollar stays at its current level. However, that probably isn't a safe assumption. By including the inflation factor, the result is an amount that anticipates ongoing inflation at the selected rate. Then, if inflation continues at that rate, the plan has some built-in safety. If the rate of inflation is higher or lower than anticipated, the income available still will be closer to what's really needed than if no inflation factor had been used at all. See Ill. 6.3 for a step-by-step explanation of the present value capital retention method.

Selecting the Contracts and Preparing the Sales Presentation

The procedures for selecting the contracts and preparing the sales presentation are the same as those you've learned in previous chapters. If you have built in an inflation factor, you may have to preplan to justify the larger amount, as we suggested earlier.

Your primary objective, of course, is to help the prospect to recognize the need for—and to purchase—the full amount. If the plan is to escape the consequences of inflation, that's what is required. If it is not possible, you may have to switch to secondary objectives and postpone certain needs until later, or reduce some of the income amounts.

For example, the dependency period income generally is considered to be the most critical. That usually should receive top priority. Perhaps some of the other needs (retirement income, for example, or the needs created by a nonworking spouse's death) can be postponed until the prospect is in a better position to do something about them. That's where ongoing service enters the picture.

Finally, because we're talking about the retention of capital in this case, you may want to assist the prospects further by suggesting some possible future uses of that capital for the children or other heirs. You also can be helpful in discussing methods for passing the capital to them through the use of wills, trusts and other devices.

With this review of capital retention methods, you now should be ready to apply them to practical situations.

■ CHAPTER 6 QUESTIONS FOR REVIEW

1. All of the following features make capital retention appealing to life insurance agents EXCEPT:

   a. service is easier and less time-consuming.
   b. it is easier to sell since relatively less capital is needed than for capital utilization.
   c. it appeals to more sophisticated people with higher incomes.
   d. planning and presentation are easier than they are with other methods.

2. What is the approximate monthly equivalent of 9 percent annual earnings?

   a. .009
   b. .06
   c. .005
   d. .0075

3. The purpose of capital retention is to create a capital fund of sufficient size to:

   a. satisfy all cash needs from the capital.
   b. satisfy all income needs from earnings on the remaining capital.
   c. pass the capital on intact to the heirs when there is no longer a need for income.
   d. All of the above

4. In the capital retention method, the income needed for the income periods following the first:

    a. is discounted to allow for the time value of money.
    b. is added to other income amounts and capitalized as a lump sum.
    c. is ignored.
    d. None of the above

5. What is the capital amount required to meet a current monthly income need of $700 using the simple method and 6 percent annual interest rate?

    a. $116,600
    b. $122,000
    c. $140,000
    d. $350,000

7

Capital Retention
Case Studies

T his chapter presents practical application of the capital retention methods learned in Chapter 6. In applying theory to practice, we'll complete two work sheets, first for a one-income family and then for a two-income family. We'll calculate the amount of new life insurance needed and discuss how and why to recommend certain products. We'll discuss living values and the additional forms and information you'll need to make the sale.

■ ■ ■ ■ ■

This chapter presents practical applications of material from the preceding chapter. We'll complete work sheets, using family situations, then make policy selections and prepare presentation forms.

Chapter 6 covered the rationale and explanations for all the material in this chapter; only new or different material is added here. If any part of the discussion seems unfamiliar, return to Chapter 6 and review that information.

■ A ONE-INCOME FAMILY CASE

You have concluded a successful fact-finding session with Steve and Kathy Brown and now wish to engineer a total needs plan using a capital retention method. The pertinent facts about this family follow.

Family Data

Steve—Age 35; good health; employed as sales vice president for Zeta, a growing company

Kathy—Age 32; good health; not employed outside the home

Children—Gary, age 9 and Heidi, age 4; both are healthy

General Financial Data

Steve—$55,500 annual salary ($4,625 per month); plans to retire at age 65

Kathy—No personal earnings and doesn't plan to work outside the home

Present General Assets—$2,000 in cash and checking account; $10,000 in E Bonds; $23,000 in stocks; $16,000 vested in pension plan

Present Liabilities—$70,000 mortgage on home

Present Life Insurance

Steve—$83,000 Group (term); $20,000 Whole Life purchased at age 26; $10,000 paid-up 20-Pay Life (purchased by parents at Steve's birth)

Kathy—No coverage

Children—$5,000 Whole Life on each

Social Security*

Steve—Fully insured; current family survivor benefit about $2,190; age-65 retirement benefit of $1,176 (reduced for early retirement) in today's dollars; $255 single-sum death benefit

Kathy—No coverage

Other Data

Veteran's Death Benefit—Steve is eligible for $150

Pension Plan—Steve is to receive about $1,600 per month at age 65

Additional Premium—Steve and Kathy could set aside an additional $280 per month, if needed

Objectives

The Browns' objectives are shown in Ill. 7.1.

■ THE WORK SHEET FOR STEVE AND KATHY BROWN

Based on the foregoing information, let's discuss the cash and income needs of the family, which are shown in the work sheet as Ill. 7.2.

---

* Assumes 1992 Social Security rates.

ILL. 7.1 ■ Objectives for Steve and Kathy Bonus

Objectives	If Steve Dies	If Kathy Dies
Cash Needs:		
Final Expenses*	$13,955	$39,000
Housing Fund	70,000	—
Education Fund	50,000	—
Monthly Income Needs:		
Dependency Period Income:		
Until *Gary* is age 18	$ 3,600/mo	$ 4,000/mo
Until *Heidi* is age 16	3,600/mo	4,000/mo
Until *Heidi* is age 18	3,600/mo	4,000/mo
Spouse's Life Income:		
To *Kathy* to age 60	$ 2,750/mo	
For life thereafter	2,750/mo	
To *Steve* to age 65		$ 4,000/mo
For life thereafter		2,750/mo
Retirement income at Steve's age 65 if both live	$4,000/mo (in terms of today's dollars or current purchasing power)	

*Although the couple felt that most final expenses might be about the same for Steve and Kathy they included an additional $25,000 "Other" in this item and higher "Income" objective if Kathy dies. These undoubtedly reflect awareness of such hidden costs as replacing the child-care and housekeeping services now performed by Kathy if she should die.

Cash Needs

If you have any problem with the Social Security and/or Other Govt. Benefits figures in the first section of the work sheet, turn back to the Cash Needs discussion in the first case study in Chapter 5.

Monthly Income Needs (In Terms of Income)

In the second section, only a few items could cause any question. First, the Social Security figure in the first column of the upper portion of this section is $2,190, or the maximum family benefit. The Social Security figure in the last column of this upper portion is $895, representing reduced survivor's benefits payable at Kathy's age 60, the earliest age she would qualify for such benefits.

Second, in the fifth column of the lower portion, "If Kathy Dies," the $1,600 *Continuing Income* figure is Steve's $1,600 pension.

As you can see, there are present income requirements only if Steve dies; therefore, we do not need to determine any capital amounts in the event of Kathy's death.

ILL. 7.2 ■ Total Needs Work Sheet (side 1)

TOTAL NEEDS WORK SHEET

CASH NEEDS

If _Steve_ Dies (Husband)   If _Kathy_ Dies (Wife)

	Objectives	S.S. and/or Other Govt. Benefits	Present Requirements	Objectives	S.S. and/or Other Govt. Benefits	Present Requirements
Final Expenses	$13,955	$405	$13,550	$39,000	$ —	$39,000
Housing Fund	70,000		70,000	—	—	—
Education Fund	50,000		50,000	—	—	—
TOTAL CASH NEEDS			**$133,550**			**$39,000**

MONTHLY INCOME NEEDS

If _Steve_ Dies (Husband)   _Kathy_'s Age (Wife)

	32 For 9 Depend. Yrs While 3 or More Elig	41 For 3 Depend. Yrs While 2 Eligible	44 For 2 Depend. Yrs While 1 Eligible	46 For 14 Yrs. Until Wife is Age 60	60 Wife for Life
Objectives	$3,600	$3,600	$3,600	$2,750	$2,750
S.S. and/or Other Govt. Benefits	2,190	1,878	939	—	895
Continuing Income (Wife)	—	—	—	—	—
Present Requirements	$1,410	$1,722	$2,661	$2,750	$1,855
Capital Amounts $ _____					
$ _____	$	$	$	$	$

If _Kathy_ Dies (Wife)   _Steve_'s Age (Husband)

	35 For 9 Depend. Yrs While 3 or More Elig	44 For 3 Depend. Yrs While 2 Eligible	47 For 2 Depend. Yrs While 1 Eligible	49 For 16 Yrs. Until Husband is Age 65	65 Husband for Life
Objectives	$4,000	$4,000	$4,000	$4,000	$2,750
S.S. and/or Other Govt. Benefits	—	—	—	—	1,176
Continuing Income (Husband)	4,625	4,625	4,625	4,625	1,600
Present Requirements	$ —	$ —	$ —	$ —	$ —
Capital Amounts $ _____					
$ _____	$	$	$	$	$

TOTAL PRESENT REQUIREMENTS

If _____ Dies $ _____ (Husband)   If _____ Dies $ _____ (Wife)

Side 1

Monthly Income Needs (In Terms of Capital)

Converting income needs into capital is where the simple method and the present value method of capital retention vary. So we'll look at each version of this step next.

The Simple Method

Illustration 7.3 shows the completed section of the work sheet using the simple method to determine the *Capital Amounts*.

The highest monthly income amount, falling in the fourth income period, is $2,750. To determine the capital amount that, at a given interest rate, will produce earnings in the amount of $2,750 per month, follow this procedure:

1. Determine the annual interest rate assumption (in this case, we assume 6 percent).
2. Divide that rate by twelve months to determine the monthly percentage:

$$.06 \div 12 = .005$$

3. Divide the needed income amount ($2,750) by .005:

$$\$2,750 \div .005 = \$550,000$$

This total represents the full capital amount, using the simple method in capital retention, to produce monthly earnings to meet the highest income need period.

ILL. 7.3 ■ Monthly Income Needs—Simple Method

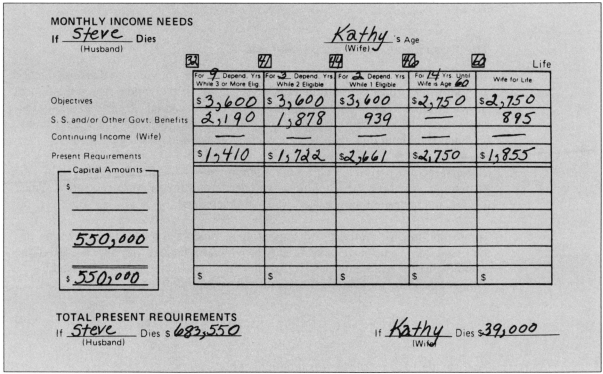

ILL. 7.4 ■ Monthly Income Needs—Present Value or Discount Method

MONTHLY INCOME NEEDS

If _Steve_ Dies
(Husband)

Kathy 's Age
(Wife)

	32	41	44	46	60	Life
	For 9 Depend. Yrs While 3 or More Elig	For 3 Depend. Yrs While 2 Eligible	For 2 Depend. Yrs While 1 Eligible	For 14 Yrs. Until Wife is Age 60	Wife for Life	
Objectives	$3,600	$3,600	$3,600	$2,750	$2,750	
S. S. and/or Other Govt. Benefits	2,190	1,878	939	—	895	
Continuing Income (Wife)	—	—	—	—	—	
Present Requirements	$1,410	$1,722	$2,661	$2,750	$1,855	
Capital Amounts						
$ 282,000	$1,410 (earn)	$1,410 (earn)	$1,410 (earn)	$1,410 (earn)	$1,410 (earn)	
36,900		312 (earn)	312 (earn)	312 (earn)	312 (earn)	
93,300			939 (earn)	939 (earn)	939 (earn)	
7,900				89 (earn)	89 (earn)	
					—	
$ 420,100	$1,410	$1,722	$2,661	$2,750	$2,750	

TOTAL PRESENT REQUIREMENTS

If _Steve_ Dies $553,650
(Husband)

If _Kathy_ Dies $39,000
(Wife)

If Steve dies, the *Total Present Requirements* (cash and income) are $683,550. This is the sum of *Total Cash Needs* ($133,550) and *Capital Amounts* ($550,000).

If Kathy dies, the *Total Present Requirements* are only $39,000, from *Total Cash Needs*.

The Present Value or Discount Method

To determine the monthly income needs using the present value or discount method, we follow the procedures outlined in the preceding chapter, and develop the figures shown in Ill. 7.4. Since only the earnings on invested capital are used to satisfy income requirements, the capital is preserved. Let's continue using the 6 percent annual interest rate in this method to determine the *Capital Amounts.*

The first income period has a present requirement of $1,410. Divide $1,410 by .005 to arrive at $282,000; the *Capital Amount* needed for the first income period. Since this amount is needed immediately, it is not discounted.

The second income period shows a monthly income need for $1,722. However, in the first income period we have already provided for capital to satisfy $1,410 of the monthly income need. Subtract the first income need from the second period income need to find the amount that requires new capital:

$$\$1,722 - \$1,410 = \$312$$

Now, divide $312 by the assumed monthly net earnings:

$$\$312 \div .005 = \$62,400$$

Since this amount is not needed immediately, discount it to its present value by using Ill. 5.20, "The Present Value (Discount) Table." In nine years, $62,400 discounted is $36,900:

$$.5919 \times \$62,400 = \$36,935$$

The third income period shows a monthly income need for $2,661. However, we have already provided for capital to satisfy $1,722 of the monthly income need. Subtract the second period income need from the third period income need to find the amount that requires new capital:

$$\$2,661 - \$1,722 = \$939$$

Now, divide $939 by the assumed monthly net earnings:

$$\$939 \div .005 = \$187,800$$

Once again, this amount is not needed immediately; therefore, discount it to its present value. In twelve years, $187,800 discounted is $93,300:

$$.4970 \times \$187,800 = \$93,337$$

The fourth income period shows a monthly income need for $2,750. However, we have already provided for capital to satisfy $2,661 of the monthly income need. Subtract the third period income need from the fourth period income need to find the amount that requires new capital:

$$\$2,750 - \$2,661 = \$89$$

Now, divide $89 by the assumed monthly net earnings:

$$\$89 \div .005 = \$17,800$$

Once again this amount is not needed immediately, therefore discount it to its present value. In 14 years, $17,800 discounted is $7,900:

$$.4423 \times \$17,800 = \$7,873$$

The last income needs period shows a need for $1,855. However, the need for this capital has been satisfied already. The Browns do not require any additional capital amounts for this income period.

The total capital required to satisfy Kathy's monthly income needs is determined by adding the *Capital Amounts* for each period: $420,100.

If Steve dies, Kathy's *Total Present Requirements* (cash and income) are $553,650. This is the sum of *Total Cash Needs* ($133,550) and *Capital Amounts* ($420,100).

If Kathy dies, Steve's *Total Present Requirements* remain at $39,000, from *Total Cash Needs.*

ILL. 7.5 ■ Present Requirements vs. Present Resources

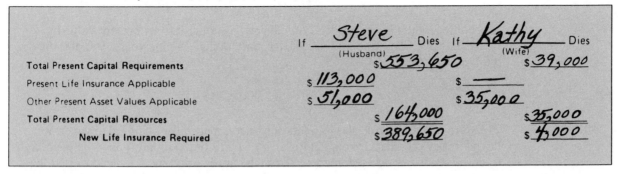

	If _Steve_ Dies	If _Kathy_ Dies
	(Husband)	(Wife)
Total Present Capital Requirements	$553,650	$39,000
Present Life Insurance Applicable	$113,000	$ ——
Other Present Asset Values Applicable	$51,000	$35,000
Total Present Capital Resources	$164,000	$35,000
New Life Insurance Required	$389,650	$4,000

Notice that Kathy's *Total Present Requirements* are $129,900 less by this method than by the simple method.

As noted there is some difference in the results obtained by the two methods. But for illustration throughout the remainder of this case study, because the remaining procedures are identical for both methods, we'll use $553,650 as the *Total Present Requirement* if Steve dies and $39,000 if Kathy dies.

New Life Insurance Required

The next step is to determine the amount of new life insurance required on the life of each spouse. We find that the next section of the work sheet is virtually self-explanatory (see Ill. 7.5).

The only explanation that might be necessary is why the *Other Present Asset Values* total is $51,000 if Steve dies, but only $35,000 if Kathy dies, The difference is the $16,000 vested in Steve's pension—available to Kathy if he dies, but not to Steve should Kathy die.

New Life Insurance Recommended

In selecting policies to satisfy the requirements in this case, use good judgment and common sense principles as described in prior case studies. For example, stay within the new premium limit of $280 per month indicated in the fact-finding session; use cash value policies to cover all death needs to the extent possible.

ILL. 7.6 ■ New Insurance Recommended

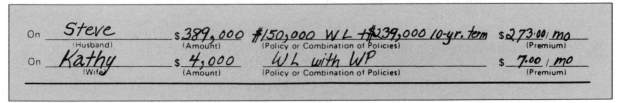

On _Steve_	$389,000	#150,000 WL + $239,000 10-yr. term	$273.00 / mo
(Husband)	(Amount)	(Policy or Combination of Policies)	(Premium)
On _Kathy_	$4,000	WL with WP	$7.00 / mo
(Wife)	(Amount)	(Policy or Combination of Policies)	(Premium)

ILL. 7.7 ■ Living Values

RETIREMENT INCOME

For _Steve_ at _65_ AND _Kathy_ at _62_ – _20—_
(Husband)   (age)   (Wife)   (age)   (year)

From:
                                                       Monthly
                                                  Life Income

Social Security and/or Other Gov't Benefits   _Steve_ (Husband) $_1,176_
                                             Kathy (Wife)   _653_

Pension and/or Profit Sharing Plans   _Steve_ (Husband)   _1,600_
                                                  (Wife)   —

                                                      Option or
                                                      Earnings Rate

Present Life Insurance   _Steve_ (Husband)   (_6% earn on CV_)   _90_
                      (Wife)   (_____)   —

New Life Insurance   _Steve_ (Husband)   (_6% earn on CV_)   _267_
                      Kathy (Wife)   (_6% earn on CV_)   _6_

Other   _$35,000 general assets_   _175_
                                    (6% earn)

Total Monthly Retirement Income $_3,967_

MISCELLANEOUS (Education, Opportunity, Emergency Funds, etc.)

If needed for education purposes, there would be approximately:

—_$50,000 at Gary's age 18 and_

—_$50,000 at Heidi's age 18_

(Any of these values used must be repaid or replaced, of course, if retirement values are to stand.)

In this case we recommend the policies shown in Ill. 7.6.* Other policies might be just as good if their selection is based on similar considerations of needs, wants, attitudes and circumstances. You may wish to consider the interest rate sensitive products.

---

* For illustration only, fictitious rates and values approximating those of nonparticipating policies, or participating policies where dividends are used to reduce the premiums, are used here and throughout this text.

This selection appears to meet the primary requirements and the total premium is within the $280 figure Steve and Kathy said they could manage.

Living Values

Now let's see how the plan stacks up regarding living values. In the *Retirement Income* portion of the work sheet, illustrated as Ill. 7.7, the first three entries are Steve's Social Security retirement benefit at age 65, Kathy's Social Security spouse's benefit at age 62 and Steve's pension. Note that Kathy's Social Security retirement benefit is reduced if she elects to receive this benefit beginning at age 62. (See the *Guide to Social Security*.)

Steve's present life insurance will have an age-65 cash value of about $18,150 ($10,660 from the $20,000 whole life and $7,520 from the $10,000 20-pay life). The assumption is that this cash value will produce net earnings of 6 percent annually or about $90 per month.

Steve's recommended new life insurance would have an age-65 cash value of about $53,550, which invested at a net 6 percent, would produce about $267 per month. Kathy's recommended new life insurance would have an age-62 cash value of about $1,290, which invested at a net 6 percent, would produce about $6 per month.

The $35,000 general assets also are assumed to be intact and invested to produce a net 6 percent, or $175 per month.

The *Total Monthly Retirement Income* falls a little short of the couple's $4,000 per month objective. However, because their planned retirement will not occur for 30 years, they have considerable time to increase their sources of retirement income. Moreover, they'll receive the $3,967 per month without drawing on capital, which they could if necessary.

■ SALES KIT

Rather than repeat previous discussions, we'll mention simply the standard items of the sales kit, in the proper order. Then, we'll examine completed presentation forms and a sample "Recommendations and Key Benefits" sheet for this case.

The standard contents are:

1. The original fact-finding form
2. The outline presentation
3. "Recommendations and Key Benefits" sheet
4. Sales wrap-up forms

The completed forms for Steve and Kathy Brown are presented as illustrations 7.8, 7.9 and 7.10.

A word of explanation about the "early capital gift possibility" in the "Recommendations and Key Benefits" sheet. The $49,100 early gift at Kathy's age 60 is simply the amount of the original $420,100 that is no longer needed to provide monthly income. Subtracting $49,100 from $420,100 leaves $371,000 in the capital account.

ILL. 7.8 ■ Total Needs Work Sheet (side 1)

PRESENT REQUIREMENTS vs. PRESENT RESOURCES

If _Steve_ Dies   If _Kathy_ Dies
(Husband)   (Wife)

Total Present Capital Requirements	$ *553,650*	$ *39,000*
Present Life Insurance Applicable	$ *113,000*	$ *—*
Other Present Asset Values Applicable	$ *51,000*	$ *35,000*
Total Present Capital Resources	$ *164,000*	$ *35,000*
New Life Insurance Required	$ *389,650*	$ *4,000*

NEW INSURANCE RECOMMENDED

On _Steve_ $ *389,000* *$150,000 WL + $239,000 10 yr. term* $ *273* /mo
(Husband)   (Amount)   (Policy or Combination of Policies)   (Premium)

On _Kathy_ $ *4,000* *WL with waiver of premiums* $ *7* /mo
(Wife)   (Amount)   (Policy or Combination of Policies)   (Premium)

LIVING VALUES

RETIREMENT INCOME

For _Steve_ at _65_ AND _Kathy_ at _62_ – _20 yr._
(Husband) (age) (Wife) (age) (year)

From:

			Monthly Life Income
Social Security and/or Other Gov't Benefits	_Steve_ (Husband)		$ *1,176*
	Kathy (Wife)		*653*
Pension and/or Profit-Sharing Plans	_Steve_ (Husband)		*1,600*
	(Wife)	Option or Earnings Rate	*—*
Present Life Insurance	_steve_ (Husband)	*(6% earn on CV)*	*90*
	(Wife)	( )	*—*
New Life Insurance	_Steve_ (Husband)	*(6% earn on CV)*	*267*
	Kathy (Wife)	*(6% earn on CV)*	*6*
Other	*$35,000 general assets (6% earn)*		*175*
Total Monthly Retirement Income			$ *3,967*

MISCELLANEOUS (Education, Opportunity, Emergency Funds, etc.)

If needed for education purposes, there would be approximately
— $50,000 at Gary's age 18 and
— $50,000 at Heidi's age 18
(Any of these values must be repaid or replaced, of course, if retirement values are to stand.)

Side 2

ILL. 7.9 ■ Total Needs Work Sheet (side 2)

TOTAL NEEDS WORK SHEET

CASH NEEDS

If _Steve_ Dies (Husband)   If _Kathy_ Dies (Wife)

	Objectives	S.S. and/or Other Govt. Benefits	Present Requirements	Objectives	S.S. and/or Other Govt. Benefits	Present Requirements
Final Expenses	$13,955	$405	$13,550	$39,000	$ —	$39,000
Housing Fund	70,000	—	70,000	—	—	—
Education Fund	50,000	—	50,000	—	—	—
TOTAL CASH NEEDS			$133,550			$39,000

MONTHLY INCOME NEEDS

If _Steve_ Dies (Husband)   _Kathy_'s Age (Wife)

	32 For 4 Depend. Yrs. While 3 or More Elig.	41 For 3 Depend. Yrs. While 2 Eligible	44 For 2 Depend. Yrs. While 1 Eligible	46 For 14 Yrs. Until Wife is Age 60	60 Wife for Life — Life
Objectives	$3,600	$3,600	$3,600	$2,750	$2,750
S.S. and/or Other Govt. Benefits	2,190	1,878	939	—	895
Continuing Income (Wife)	—			—	—
Present Requirements	$1,410	$1,722	$2,661	$2,750	$1,855
Capital Amounts $282,000	$1,410 (earn)	$1,410 (earn)	$1,410 (earn)	$1,410 (earn)	$1,410 (earn)
36,900		312 (earn)	312 (earn)	312 (earn)	312 (earn)
93,300			939 (earn)	939 (earn)	939 (earn)
7,900				89 (earn)	89 (earn)
$420,100	$1,410	$1,722	$2,661	$2,750	$2,750

If _Kathy_ Dies (Wife)   _Steve_'s Age (Husband)

	39 For 4 Depend. Yrs. While 3 or More Elig.	44 For 3 Depend. Yrs While 2 Eligible	47 For 2 Depend. Yrs While 1 Eligible	49 For 16 Yrs. Until Husband is Age 65	65 Husband for Life — Life
Objectives	$4,000	$4,000	$4,000	$4,000	$2,750
S.S. and/or Other Govt. Benefits	—	—	—	—	1,176
Continuing Income (Husband)	4,625	4,625	4,625	4,625	1,600
Present Requirements	$ —	$ —	$ —	$ —	$ —
Capital Amounts $					
$	$	$	$	$	$

TOTAL PRESENT REQUIREMENTS
If _Steve_ Dies $553,650 (Husband)   If _Kathy_ Dies $39,000 (Wife)

Side 1

ILL. 7.10 ■ Family Financial Summary

PREPARED FOR: *Steve and Kathy*   DATE: *1/8*

FAMILY FINANCIAL SUMMARY

	For *Kathy* (Wife) if *Steve* (Husband) should die.		For *Steve* (Husband) if *Kathy* (Wife) should die.	
CASH NEEDS				
Final Expenses Objective	$ *13,955*		$ *39,000*	
Less Social Security and/or Other Govt. Benefits	$ *405*		$ —	
Present Requirement		$ *13,550*		$ *39,000*
Your Housing Fund — Present Requirement		$ *70,000*		
Your Children's Education — Objective	$ *50,000*		$ —	
Less Social Security and/or Other Govt. Benefits	$ —		$ —	
Present Requirement		$ *50,000*		$ —
Total Cash Needs		$ *133,550*		$ *39,000*
MONTHLY INCOME NEEDS				
Dependency Period — 3 or more eligible — Objective	$ *3,600*		$ *4,000*	
Less Social Security and/or Other Govt. Benefits	$ *2,190*		$ —	
Less Continuing Personal Income	$ —		$ *4,625*	
Present Requirement (Income—Capital)	$ *1,410*	– $ *282,000*	$ —	– $ —
Dependency Period — 2 eligible — Objective	$ *3,600*		$ *4,000*	
Less Social Security and/or Other Govt. Benefits	$ *1,878*		$ —	
Less Continuing Personal Income	$ —		$ *4,625*	
Present Requirement (Income—Capital)	$ *1,722*	– $ *36,900*	$ —	– $ —
Dependency Period — 1 eligible — Objective	$ *3,600*		$ *4,000*	
Less Social Security and/or Other Govt. Benefits	$ *939*		$ —	
Less Continuing Personal Income	$ —		$ *4,625*	
Present Requirement (Income—Capital)	$ *2,661*	– $ *93,300*	$ —	– $ —
For spouse (no children) — Objective — to Age	$ *2,750* *60*		$ *4,000* *65*	
Less Continuing Personal Income	$ —		$ *4,625*	
Present Requirement (Income—Capital)	$ *2,750*	– $ *7,900*	$ —	– $ —
For spouse (no children) — Objective — for Life After Age	$ *2,750* *60*		$ *2,750* *65*	
Less Social Security and/or Other Govt. Benefits	$ *895*		$ *1,176*	
Less Continuing Personal Income	$ —		$ *1,600*	
Present Requirement (Income—Capital)	$ *1,855*	– $ —	$ —	– $ —
Total Capital to Satisfy Income Needs		$ *420,100*		$ —
Total Capital to Satisfy Cash and Income Needs		$ *553,650*		$ *39,000*
Less Existing Life Insurance and Other Assets		$ *164,000*		$ *35,000*
Amount Still Required to Satisfy Your Objectives		$ *389,650*		$ *4,000*

RECOMMENDATIONS: *New Life Insurance of:*

$389,000 on Steve — $150,000 WL + $239,000 10-yr. term   *$273/mo*
convert and renew all with WP

$4,000 on Kathy — $4,000 WL with WP   *7/mo*

                            $280/mo

RETIREMENT INCOME if you live, starting at *Steve* (Husband) 's age *65* and *Kathy* (Wife) 's age *62*:

From Social Security and/or Other Government Benefit Plans	$ *1,829*
From Present Insurance, Employee Retirement Plans and Other Resources	$ *1,865*
From Recommended New Life Insurance	$ *273*
Total Retirement Income	$ *3,967*

ILL. 7.11 ■ Recommendations and Key Benefits

A. POLICY RECOMMENDATIONS

To provide the additional capital required to satisfy your family financial objectives completely if either of you should not live, it is recommended that you purchase additional life insurance as follows:

On Steve's life—

$389,000:	$150,000 Whole Life at $188 per month and $239,000 10-Year Term (convertible and renewable) at $85 per month, all with Waiver of Premium	Monthly Premium	$273

On Kathy's life—

$4,000 Whole Life with Waiver of Premium

Monthly Premium	$ 7
Total New Monthly Premium	$280

B. RETIREMENT INCOME

If the recommended program is adopted, your monthly retirement income at Steve's age 65 and Kathy's age 62 will be as follows:

From Steve's Social Security coverage (for you both)	$1,829
From Steve's present insurance and pension plan	1,690
From Steve's recommended new life insurance	267
From Kathy's recommended new life insurance	6
From other liquid assets	175
Total monthly retirement income	$3,967*

*If desired, some paid-up life insurance may be elected on either Steve or Kathy, or both, in lieu of some income at retirement. Each $1,000 of paid-up insurance would call for an income reduction of about $3 per month.

C. EDUCATION FUNDS

Substantial funds have been provided in this plan for the education of Gary and Heidi in event of Steve's death. But what if Steve lives? The recommended program will make education funds available as follows:

	At Gary's Age 18	AND	At Heidi's Age 18
From loans on present insurance†	$ 6,225		$ 6,225
From loans on new insurance†	26,775		26,775
From other liquid assets (estimate)	17,000		17,000
Total funds available	$50,000	AND	$50,000

†Any values used for educational purposes must be repaid or replaced, of course, if the above retirement income is to be available.

D. EARLY CAPITAL GIFT POSSIBILITY

In the unfortunate event of Steve's early death, a surplus of capital required to satisfy your objectives would arise after your youngest child attains age 18. Accordingly, if desired, the following early capital gift could be made without shorting your stated objectives:

To Gary and Heidi after Kathy's attainment of age 60, a total gift of $49,100

The remaining $371,000 would be retained after Kathy's age 60, however, and not passed until after her life income objective had been fully satisfied.

$$\$420,100 - \$49,100 = \$371,000$$

That amount multiplied by the .005 assumed monthly earnings equals \$1,855, the monthly income requirement for Kathy when she reaches age 60.

$$\$371,000 \times .005 = \$1,855$$

When the completed presentation form and this "Recommendations and Key Benefits" sheet are sandwiched between the original fact-finding form and the appropriate sales wrap-up forms, the sales kit is ready. It provides the basis for a very effective total needs selling presentation and greatly enhances the odds of a successful close.

■ A TWO-INCOME FAMILY CASE

The capital retention method also works well in a two-income family situation. Because the procedures and rationale are nearly the same as for one-income situations, we won't include lengthy explanations. Instead, we'll examine a typical two-income family and study the work sheet and presentation forms. Our two-income family is headed by Jim and Terri Black.

Family Data

Jim—Age 30; good health; junior executive with a promising future; assumes about 25 percent of housekeeping chores

Terri—Age 30; good health; professional; assumes about 25 percent of child-care and housekeeping responsibilities—remaining 50 percent of child-care and housekeeping chores handled by hired help

Children—Laurie, age 7; good health

General Financial Data

Jim—\$42,000 annual salary (\$3,500 per month); plans to retire at age 65

Terri—\$30,000 annual salary (\$2,500 per month); plans to retire at age 65

Present General Assets—\$3,000 cash and checking; \$12,500 in savings and other liquid assets

Present Liabilities—\$60,000 mortgage on home; \$4,000 other loans

Present Life Insurance

Jim—\$54,000 Group (term); \$3,500 Whole Life purchased at age 26

Terri—\$45,000 Group (term); \$2,000 paid-up 20-Pay Life (purchased by parents at age 4)

Children—\$2,000 Whole Life on Laurie

ILL. 7.12 ■ Objectives for Jim and Terri Black

Objectives	If Jim Dies	If Terri Dies
Cash Needs:		
Final Expenses	$10,555	$ 9,555
Housing Fund*	36,000 (60%)	24,000 (40%)
Education Fund	25,000	25,000
Monthly Income Needs:		
Dependency Period Income:		
Until *Laurie* is age 18	$ 4,000/mo	$ 4,000/mo
Spouse's Life Income:		
To *Terri* to age 65	$ 3,000/mo	
For life thereafter	3,000/mo	
To *Jim* to age 65		$ 3,000/mo
For life thereafter		3,000/mo
Retirement income at Jim's and Terri's age 65 if both live	$4,000/mo (in terms of today's dollars or current purchasing power)	

*Responsibility for the mortgage is divided between the spouses in the approximate ratios as their respective incomes bear to their combined income (60%/40%).

Social Security*

Jim—Fully insured; present credited earnings would produce a current family survivor benefit of $1,662 (reduced to $831 if Terri continues to work); projected credited earnings to age 65 would produce a reduced personal retirement benefit of $993 per month, based on today's dollar values

Terri—Fully insured; present credited earnings would produce a current survivor benefit of $1,450 (reduced to $725 if Jim continues to work); projected credited earnings to age 65 would produce a reduced retirement benefit of $863 per month, in terms of today's dollars

Other Data

Pension Plan—Jim will receive $245 a month at age 65; Terri will receive $185 a month at age 65

Additional Premium—The Blacks could set aside an additional $400 per month, if needed

Objectives

The objectives of the Blacks are shown in Ill. 7.12.

---

* Assumes 1992 Social Security rates.

ILL. 7.13 ■ Total Needs Work Sheet (side 1)

TOTAL NEEDS WORK SHEET

CASH NEEDS

If ___Jim___ Dies (Husband)   If ___Terri___ Dies (Wife)

	Objectives	S.S. and/or Other Govt. Benefits	Present Requirements	Objectives	S.S. and/or Other Govt. Benefits	Present Requirements
Final Expenses	$10,555	$255	$10,300	$9,555	$255	$9,300
Housing Fund	36,000	—	36,000	24,000	—	24,000
Education Fund	25,000	—	25,000	25,000	—	25,000
TOTAL CASH NEEDS			$71,300	TOTAL CASH NEEDS		$58,300

MONTHLY INCOME NEEDS

If ___Jim___ Dies (Husband)   ___Terri___'s Age (Wife)

☐ ☐ ☒ 30 ☒ 41 ☒ 65   Life

	For ___ Depend. Yrs. While 3 or More Elig.	For ___ Depend. Yrs. While 2 Eligible	For _11_ Depend. Yrs. While 1 Eligible	For _24_ Yrs. Until Wife is Age _65_	Wife for Life
Objectives	$	$	$4,000	$3,000	$3,000
S.S. and/or Other Govt. Benefits			831	—	1,108
Continuing Income (Wife)			2,500	2,500	185
Present Requirements	$	$	$669	$500	$1,707

Capital Amounts
$_____
_____
_____
_____
341,400
$341,400

$	$	$	$	$	

If ___Terri___ Dies (Wife)   ___Jim___'s Age (Husband)

☐ ☐ ☒ 30 ☒ 41 ☒ 65   Life

	For ___ Depend. Yrs While 3 or More Elig	For ___ Depend. Yrs While 2 Eligible	For _11_ Depend. Yrs. While 1 Eligible	For _24_ Yrs. Until Husband is Age _65_	Husband for Life
Objectives	$	$	$4,000	$3,000	$3,000
S.S. and/or Other Govt. Benefits			725	—	993
Continuing Income (Husband)			3,500	3,500	245
Present Requirements	$	$	$ —	$ —	$1,762

Capital Amounts
$_____
_____
_____
_____
352,400
$352,400

$	$	$	$	$	

TOTAL PRESENT REQUIREMENTS

If ___Jim___ Dies $412,700 (Husband)   If ___Terri___ Dies $410,700 (Wife)

Side 1

ILL. 7.14 ■ Total Needs Work Sheet (side 2)

PRESENT REQUIREMENTS vs. PRESENT RESOURCES

If __Jim__ Dies   If __Terri__ Dies
(Husband)   (Wife)

	If Jim Dies	If Terri Dies
Total Present Capital Requirements	$ 412,700	$ 410,700
Present Life Insurance Applicable	$ 59,000	$ 47,000
Other Present Asset Values Applicable	$ 15,500	$ 15,500
Total Present Capital Resources	$ 74,500	$ 62,500
New Life Insurance Required	$ 338,200	$ 348,200

NEW INSURANCE RECOMMENDED

On		Amount	Policy or Combination of Policies	Premium
__Jim__ (Husband)		$ 338,200	$200,000 WL + $ 138,000 10-yr. term	$ 220 / mo
__Terri__ (Wife)		$ 348,000	$200,000 WL + $ 148,000 10-yr. term	$ 180 / mo

LIVING VALUES

RETIREMENT INCOME

For __Jim__ at __65__ AND __Terri__ at __65__ — __20—__
(Husband)   (age)   (Wife)   (age)   (year)

From:

		Option or Earnings Rate	Monthly Life Income
Social Security and/or Other Gov't Benefits	Jim (Husband)		$ 993
	Terri (Wife)		863
Pension and/or Profit Sharing Plans	Jim (Husband)		245
	Terri (Wife)		185
Present Life Insurance	Jim (Husband)	(___)	11
	Terri (Wife)	(___)	6
New Life Insurance	Jim (Husband)	(___)	332
	Terri (Wife)	(___)	332
Other	$15,500 present liquid assets		65
Total Monthly Retirement Income			$ 3,032

MISCELLANEOUS (Education, Opportunity, Emergency Funds, etc.)

If needed for education purposes, there would be approximately:
— $40,000 at Laura's age 18

(Any of these values must be repaid or replaced,
of course, if retirement values are to stand.)

Side 2

■ THE WORK SHEET FOR JIM AND TERRI BLACK

The work sheet for Jim and Terri is shown as Ill. 7.12. Assume a 6 percent annual earnings rate or .005 monthly (.06 ÷ 12 months = .005).

The work sheet is based on the simple method because this couple doesn't have enough present liquid assets to justify use of the present value method. Unless one of the spouses died immediately, there would not be enough present capital exclusive of life insurance to equal the future capital requirement when it arrived.

Remember that, as mentioned earlier, any capital that is no longer needed to satisfy subsequent income objectives may be given to children or others at that time. Early transfers can offer such advantages as tax savings and the pleasure of actually seeing the donee's appreciation for the gift.

■ SALES KIT

The sales kit for this case should include the same items in the same order as discussed previously.

The "Family Financial Summary" presentation form (see Ill. 7.15) requires no explanations beyond those given earlier. Everything is picked up directly or indirectly from the work sheet or discussions relating to it.

The only item missing from this "Recommendations and Key Benefits" sheet (see Ill. 7.16) that may need additional explanation are the early capital gift possibilities. Because the larger *Present Requirements* regarding income fall in the later income periods in the event of Terri's or Jim's early death, not much opportunity for early gifts of capital can be foreseen at this time.

When all of the forms are put in order, the sales kit is ready. The presentation and closing session should move smoothly and effectively with substantial opportunity for a resulting sale.

This concludes our capital retention case studies. It also concludes our examination of all total needs selling methods and examples, both capital utilization and capital retention. All that remains is "Wrapping Up the Sale," which is the title of our next chapter.

■ CHAPTER 7 QUESTIONS FOR REVIEW

1. The sales kit contains all of the following EXCEPT:
   a. policy forms.
   b. fact-finding form.
   c. sales wrap-up forms.
   d. outline presentation.

ILL. 7.15 ■ Family Financial Summary

PREPARED FOR: *Jim and Terri* DATE: *1/12*

FAMILY FINANCIAL SUMMARY

	For *Terri* (Wife) if *Jim* (Husband) should die.		For *Jim* (Husband) if *Terri* (Wife) should die.	
CASH NEEDS				
Final Expenses Objective	$ *10,555*		$ *9,555*	
Less Social Security and/or Other Govt. Benefits	$ *255*		$ *255*	
Present Requirement		$ *10,300*		$ *9,300*
Your Housing Fund – Present Requirement		$ *36,000*		$ *24,000*
Your Children's Education – Objective	$ *25,000*		$ *25,000*	
Less Social Security and/or Other Govt. Benefits	$ *—*		$ *—*	
Present Requirement		$ *25,000*		$ *25,000*
Total Cash Needs		$ *71,300*		$ *58,300*
MONTHLY INCOME NEEDS				
Dependency Period – 3 or more eligible – Objective	$ *—*		$ *—*	
Less Social Security and/or Other Govt. Benefits	$ *—*		$ *—*	
Less Continuing Personal Income	$ *—*		$ *—*	
Present Requirement (Income–Capital)	$ *—* – $ *—*		$ *—* – $ *—*	
Dependency Period – 2 eligible – Objective	$ *—*		$ *—*	
Less Social Security and/or Other Govt. Benefits	$ *—*		$ *—*	
Less Continuing Personal Income	$ *—*		$ *—*	
Present Requirement (Income–Capital)	$ *—* – $ *—*		$ *—* – $ *—*	
Dependency Period – 1 eligible – Objective	$ *4,000*		$ *4,000*	
Less Social Security and/or Other Govt. Benefits	$ *831*		$ *725*	
Less Continuing Personal Income	$ *2,500*		$ *3,500*	
Present Requirement (Income–Capital)	$ *669* – $ *—*		$ *—* – $ *—*	
For spouse (no children) – Objective	$ *3,000*		$ *3,000*	
– to Age	*65*		*65*	
Less Continuing Personal Income	$ *2,500*		$ *3,500*	
Present Requirement (Income–Capital)	$ *500* – $ *—*		$ *—* – $ *—*	
For spouse (no children) – Objective	$ *3,000*		$ *3,000*	
– for Life After Age	*65*		*65*	
Less Social Security and/or Other Govt. Benefits	$ *1,108*		$ *993*	
Less Continuing Personal Income	$ *185*		$ *245*	
Present Requirement (Income–Capital)	$ *1,707* – $ *344,400*		$ *1,762* – $ *352,400*	
Total Capital to Satisfy Income Needs		$ *341,400*		$ *352,400*
Total Capital to Satisfy Cash and Income Needs		$ *412,700*		$ *410,700*
Less Existing Life Insurance and Other Assets		$ *74,500*		$ *62,500*
Amount Still Required to Satisfy Your Objectives		$ *338,200*		$ *348,200*

RECOMMENDATIONS: *New Life Insurance of:*

$338,000 on Jim — $200,000 WL + $138,000 10-yr. term $220/mo

$348,000 on Terri — $200,000 WL + $148,000 10-yr. term 180/mo

$400/mo

RETIREMENT INCOME if you live, starting at *Jim* (Husband) 's age *65* and *Terri* (Wife) 's age *65*:

From Social Security and/or Other Government Benefit Plans	$ *1,856*
From Present Insurance, Employee Retirement Plans, and Other Resources	$ *512*
From Recommended New Life Insurance	$ *664*
Total Retirement Income	$ *3,032*

ILL. 7.16 ■ Recommendations and Key Benefits

A. POLICY RECOMMENDATIONS

To provide the additional capital required to satisfy your family financial objectives completely if either of you should not live, it is recommended that you purchase additional life insurance as follows:

On Jim's life—

$338,000:	$200,000 Whole Life at $185 per month and $138,000 10-year Term (convertible and renewable) at $35 per month, all with Waiver of Premiums		
		Monthly Premium	$220

On Terri's life—

$348,000:	$200,000 Whole Life at $143 per month and $148,000 10-year Term (convertible and renewable) at $37 per month, all with Waiver of Premiums		
		Monthly Premium	$180
		Total New Monthly Premium	$400

B. RETIREMENT INCOME

If the recommended program is adopted, your monthly retirement income at both spouses' age 65 will be as follows:

From Jim's own Social Security coverage (in terms of today's dollars)	$ 993
From Terri's own Social Security coverage (in terms of today's dollars)	863
From Jim's present insurance and pension plan	256
From Terri's present insurance and pension plan	191
From Jim's recommended new life insurance	332
From Terri's recommended new life insurance	332
From other liquid assets	65
Total combined monthly retirement income	$3,032*

*If desired, some paid-up life insurance may be elected on either or both spouses in lieu of some income at retirement. Each $1,000 of paid-up insurance would call for an income reduction of about $3 per month.

C. EDUCATION FUNDS

Substantial funds have been provided in this plan for the education of Laurie in the event of Jim's or Terri's death. But what if both parents live? The recommended program will make education funds available as follows:

	At Laurie's Age 18
From loans on present insurance†	$ 1,215
From loans on new insurance†	34,285
From other liquid assets (estimate)†	4,500
Total funds available	$40,000

†Any values used for educational purposes must be repaid or replaced, of course, if the above retirement income is to be available.

2. If present liquid assets are relatively low, the total needs selling method used should be:

   a. simple capital retention.
   b. capital utilization.
   c. present value capital retention.
   d. single need utilization.

3. Your client is convinced he can earn 8 percent annual return on capital. What is the approximate monthly equivalent of 8 percent?

   a. .005
   b. .00417
   c. .00667
   d. .008

4. Using the simple method, what is the *Capital Amount* for the *Present Requirement* of $1,050 at 6 percent annual return?

   a. $205,000
   b. $210,000
   c. $314,800
   d. None of the above

5. You have already determined the *Capital Amount* required for the first income period using the present value or discount method of capital retention. The *Present Requirement* for the first income period is $1,707 and for the second income period it is $1,978. Which of the following numbers would you use to calculate the *Capital Amount* for the second income period?

   a. $271
   b. $1,707
   c. $1,978
   d. None of the above

8

Wrapping Up the Sale

T o help you finalize the sale, this chapter gives you specific sales ideas that work especially well in total needs selling. You'll learn how to follow-through by obtaining new insurance and setting up plan specifics and settlement directions. Helpful hints show you how to prepare yourself and your client for the delivery interview. Critical follow-up contacts are explained and the Appendix gives you a sample financial plan format.

■ ■ ■ ■ ■

We have examined the first two phases of a sound total needs selling system: (1) fact-finding and (2) engineering the plan. The final phase, wrapping up the sale, consists of four major steps: presentation and closing, follow-through, delivery and continuing service.

■ PRESENTATION AND CLOSING

This step involves the selling session, as well as completing the application and attending to other necessary details.

The Selling Session

In total needs selling, the selling session is no different from any other well-organized selling interview. We assume that you already have the basic selling techniques and closing skills; so the discussion is limited to some additional ideas and suggestions that may prove particularly helpful in total needs selling.

Here, as always, the idea is to lead the prospect from a consideration of the need or problem to a sound solution resulting in a natural and unforced close. There is, however, one important difference. In total needs selling, you've had an earlier fact-finding interview to evaluate not only pertinent financial information but also the prospects themselves. That makes it easier to prepare the presentation. In short, conditions for selling are nearly ideal.

Practical Sales Ideas

Let's review some specific sales ideas that are especially adaptable to total needs selling. They've been adopted from the sales methods of successful life insurance agents. Together with techniques that you're now using effectively, these ideas can provide the foundation for a successful selling interview.

Review Objectives

Sometimes prospects cool off considerably between interviews. To warm them up again, you may have to reawaken concern about their families' financial needs and objectives. To do this—and also to build a natural bridge between the fact-finding session and the selling interview—it's a good idea to review their objectives carefully and to confirm that the amounts are appropriate. A straightforward question may be: "Has anything happened since our last visit to make it possible for you to reduce any of these objectives?" Usually the answer is "no." If it isn't, it's far better to uncover any uncertainty on this score early in the interview.

Focus Family's Objectives

In presenting the plan, an effective technique is to postulate that death already has occurred. You might say to either spouse: "Let's suppose that you died last night. Here is what your survivors would begin to receive today . . . ." You can then go on to point out any deficiency in meeting financial objectives. By taking the prospect out of the picture in this way, it's possible to bring the family's problems into focus.

Sell to Emotions

Throughout the interview, try to avoid discussing technicalities or giving a detailed explanation of the procedure used to determine needs. Conversation along these lines tends to divert attention away from solutions to the fundamental problems. Remember that feelings of love and concern generally are what prompt the decision to buy.

Disturb the Prospect

Obvious external pressure is apt to backfire in total needs selling. There is pressure in the interview, but it comes from the prospect's needs and problems—not from you. After pinpointing the difference between the amount required and the amount presently provided, it's often best to say nothing further. The problem, after all, is strictly the prospect's, and the prospect is entitled to be disturbed by it without outside interference. Eventually, the prospect is likely to ask for suggestions. When that happens, the sale will be made.

Make Prospect Responsible for Decision

A few prospects will balk at buying and seem to have inexhaustible reservoirs of excuses. In such situations, you can get the discussions back to reality by giving the prospects a pen and inviting them to cut down on their families's financial objectives where they see fit. This puts the responsibility squarely where it belongs.

Encourage Spouses To Explain

In a joint interview with a married couple, it can be effective to ask one of them to explain the plan to the other. This gives each an opportunity to participate fully in the discussion and to respond as if he or she were buying, rather than being sold. Couples who accept this invitation sell themselves more completely by describing the plan.

Keep It Simple

An alternative solution sometimes may be advisable, but don't mention it unless it's necessary to keep the case alive. Offering too many choices only increases the chance of indecision. When it becomes necessary to present the alternate plan, be sure to indicate which benefits have been eliminated as a result of the premium reduction. This keeps the door open for the next sale.

Close on a Minor Point

Lastly in many cases, after making your presentation and getting the prospect's approval, you can close smoothly by leading into a discussion of the flexibility incorporated in the finished plan. This technique involves a rather sophisticated application of "closing on a minor point." In effect, it gives prospects a chance to indicate that they are ready to buy without ever stating a major decision.

The Question of Flexibility

You need a clear indication of the prospect's preferences to complete the promised service. Basically, the point to be resolved is whether the survivor has the financial experience and maturity to use good judgment while handling large amounts of money. If so, the final plan usually should possess maximum flexibility. However, there may be a few exceptional cases where a fixed income plan is necessary.

The main purpose of the selling session is to close the sale. Everything else is secondary. Don't hesitate to defer the question of flexibility until later if the subject would lead the interview away from its goal. You always can discuss the matter later.

Completing the Application

The procedure of completing the application in total needs selling is virtually identical to other types of life insurance selling. We assume that you already have such skills, so we won't focus on that procedure.

Incidentally, although the policyowner should make beneficiary designations at this time, he or she should reserve the right to change them, at least for now. That will facilitate making any necessary changes when the plan specifics are actually determined.

Necessary Details

After the application and appropriate supplements have been completed and signed—and arrangements made for obtaining any additional medical information, etc.—you should carry out two other important details before ending this session.

1. Ask the policyowner of each policy involved in the plan to sign a separate letter or form for each policy, authorizing you to act as the policyowner's representative when servicing that policy. An example of a typical *Policy Service Request* is included later as Ill. 8.1.

2. Pick up the present policies involved in the plan and give each policyowner a receipt. If the policies are not available immediately, arrange to obtain them as soon as possible. You'll need them to determine plan specifics and to complete the plan summary and audit. The receipt needn't be too formal, but it should show the policy number, issuing company, kind of contract and face amount of each policy.

■ FOLLOW-THROUGH

After the plan and new insurance are sold, you are obligated to follow-through and complete all required service work. At the very minimum, that includes making sure the new insurance is obtained, that all policies are consistent with the plan and that both plan and policies are complete and understood. The ultimate rewards for conscientious service include quality referrals and repeat business that more than justify the time and effort involved.

Obtain New Insurance

The first step is to get the new insurance in force as quickly as possible. The plan is based upon utilization of all contemplated resources, including the new insurance. Promptly:

1. submit the application and any appropriate supplements after checking them carefully for full and accurate completion and
2. check the newly issued policy when it arrives to make sure it coincides with the plan as applied for.

Establish Plan Specifics

Immediately after the new insurance goes into force, establish the specifics of the plan and have any other policy provision changes or additions made. Let's consider each of several important facets.

Determine Use of Each Resource

In the "engineering the plan" phase, no attention was given to how each resource should be applied in the final plan. Although there may have been some thoughts along this line, they were premature until the required new resources had been obtained.

Each policy and each other asset now must be carefully used where it will best serve the plan—to satisfy cash needs, short-term income needs, long-term income needs and so on. To make these judgments, you must examine each resource for the following information:

1. Life insurance policies:
   a. Guaranteed interest and current excess interest factors
   b. Settlement options available
   c. Special features or current practices available
   d. Details pertaining to dividends, if participating
2. Other assets:
   a. Degree of liquidity or ease of liquidation

      b. Earnings probabilities—short-term and long-term
      c. Growth potential
      d. Special features or aspects
      e. Relative degree of safety

Based on this information you must prepare the actual plan of distribution. Prepare the plan summary for presentation during the delivery interview. Also, a distribution plan will be a helpful guide to survivors if an insured dies. Even more importantly, a distribution plan determines settlement directions, beneficiary designations and any other important provisions. Even when the plan involves use of policy proceeds to satisfy cash needs or to purchase other income-producing investments, it is wise to set up settlement directions. They may provide appropriate flexibility with withdrawal privileges yet keep the door open for use of settlement options, if necessary, when the time comes.

For determining plan specifics, the following general guidelines regarding the use of life insurance proceeds should be helpful. They are especially important when using the capital utilization methods but even for capital retention plans, these guidelines can provide additional flexibility and safety.

1. Use policies with higher guaranteed interest rates and income factors for long-term needs and deferred income provisions. This assures that maximum advantage will be available from guaranteed interest. However, that excess interest serves as an equalizer in this respect, even where there is a substantial difference in guaranteed rates.
2. Avoid splitting the proceeds of a single policy to cover more than one need except where absolutely necessary. If possible, confine such splitting to larger policies.
3. Use reducing term insurance only for needs that will decline in amount over time—e.g., the mortgage fund.
4. Use smaller policies for cash needs, unless monthly option rates are exceptionally favorable. Many companies require that the incomes payable must equal at least $10 to $20 to be paid monthly. Otherwise, payments will be made quarterly or even less frequently.
5. Use group insurance to provide cash funds unless a full selection of settlement options is available. Even then, avoid using group insurance for long-term needs. With many companies, proceeds of group insurance cannot be distributed under settlement options or restrictions will be imposed.

The use of other assets in the plan should follow common sense guidelines:

1. earmark liquid assets for cash needs;
2. earmark sound, substantial income-producing assets for income needs—normally, marginal income needs in capital utilization plans and general income needs in capital retention plans and
3. generally, consider early liquidation of speculative and low-yielding assets to (a) satisfy cash needs, (b) purchase annuities or (c) reinvest in sound, substantial income-producing assets.

Determine Settlement Directions

This determination is affected by whether the capital utilization or capital retention method is used, as well as the degree of flexibility desired. If the most flexible arrangement is desirable, place the policies under the "interest option" with an unlimited privilege to withdraw principal as needed and to change to any other option at any time.

Then prepare a letter of instructions, outlining specific settlement options to be elected or withdrawals and reinvestments to be made at the insured's death. This letter also should provide instructions regarding any other resources in the plan. Of course, it must be revised periodically with the rest of the plan.

The interest option with unrestricted withdrawal and change of option privileges has several advantages. It gives a surviving spouse time to elect settlement options or withdrawals and reinvestments. Yet cash is available immediately if needed for expenses. Furthermore, in contrast to a single-sum settlement, an automatic hedge is provided against the "common disaster" problem. From a psychological standpoint, it's probably true that the beneficiary is less likely to dissipate proceeds held on deposit.

In the exceptional situation where a spouse's financial inexperience calls for a less flexible, fixed income arrangement, it may be desirable to elect settlement options to conform more precisely with the final distribution plan. Even with a fixed income program, however, it's best to avoid complete inflexibility. This can be done by including definite annual withdrawal privileges or specific powers to change from one option to another.

A trust may be the ideal arrangement when flexibility, control and money management expertise are desired. Excellent materials on the use of such trusts are readily available.

Determine Beneficiary Designations

Next, determine the beneficiary designations that will cause the proceeds of each policy to flow according to the plan. The following suggestions may be helpful:

1. In providing for final expenses, the spouse usually is named primary beneficiary. The insured's estate or executor should be made the secondary beneficiary instead of minor children. Generally, the guardian may not use a minor child's funds to pay the deceased's final expenses.
2. As for the mortgage fund and emergency fund, naming the spouse as primary beneficiary and the children as secondary beneficiaries is common practice. The same arrangement is practical for the education fund. College funds should not be "locked up" by naming the children as primary beneficiaries because such funds might be needed for unforeseen emergencies before the children are ready for college.
3. For income purposes, the spouse usually is named primary beneficiary and the children, individually, are named secondary beneficiaries. Avoid possible disinheritance of an unnamed child; insert such a qualification as: ". . . and any other children of the insured, equally, survivors or survivor."

Check Other Important Provisions

This is also the time to check each policy to see that important provisions are included. If not, have them added. Among the provisions to be checked:

1. *Automatic premium loan provision*—to make the policies lapse-proof.

2. *Common disaster clause*—to prevent needless delays in distributing proceeds to children if the surviving spouse should die shortly after the insured.
3. *Spendthrift clause*—to put proceeds beyond the reach of the beneficiary's creditors.
4. *Premium waiver provision*—to protect the insurance in case of the insured's disability.

You also should check for any restrictions or ratings for aviation, occupation, etc., that might be removed because of subsequent changes in the policyowner's situation or current company policy.

Submit Policy Service Request Forms

Having prepared the distribution plan and made all the determinations required to implement it, you now should write to the various insurance companies requesting that settlement provisions be prepared for the policyowner's signature. In general these requests should be kept as simple as possible, stating specifically which settlement options are to apply.

Shown in Ill. 8.1 is a *Policy Service Request* form. Note that the requests are specific and uncomplicated. If other changes or additions are needed, a request for forms required to effect such changes or additions may be noted on this form and the issuing company usually will oblige.

If you promptly send the *Policy Service Request* forms, the company promptly should return the forms to you for the insureds' signatures. Carefully examine the forms to be sure they provide the appropriate information. For policies issued by your own company, you should have prepared the company's service forms. Include all of the above forms in the delivery kit for review during the delivery interview.

■ DELIVERY OF POLICIES

All of the policies involved in the plan should be included in the delivery kit so that you may refer to them firsthand during the delivery interview. Many agents like to present policy wallets, housing all policies, to their total needs clients.

Prepare Your Client

After submitting applications, successful agents immediately send notes to their applicants, thanking them for the business and briefly summarizing the general purpose of the plan and new insurance as agreed upon in the selling interview.

After the new policies arrive, check them promptly and call the clients to arrange delivery interview appointments. Use these guidelines:

1. make the appointment far enough in advance to allow ample time for making all delivery preparations;
2. arrange for enough time to permit a proper delivery interview;
3. include both spouses in the delivery interview when appropriate — this is absolutely necessary in the case of a two-income family and
4. set up the appointment at a convenient time and place that will be free of interruptions.

ILL. 8.1 ▪ Policy Service Request

POLICY SERVICE REQUEST

Date:

To:

(Company)

Re: Policy No.

Please prepare for signature the forms necessary to effect settlement of the above policy as closely as possible to the requests below:

		Relationship	Date of
I. Beneficiaries	**Name**	**to Insured**	**Birth**

   A. Primary:
   B. Secondary:
   C. Contingent:
   D. Final Reversion: Upon death of last surviving beneficiary, subsequent to death of insured, to estate of such last survivor

II. Method of Settlement (Option, frequency and duration of payments)

   A. Primary Beneficiary:
   B. Secondary Beneficiaries:
      1. Primary beneficiary predeceases insured:
      2. Primary beneficiary dies while policy proceeds are still on deposit:
      3. Primary beneficiary dies while receiving payments:

Add Noncommutable, Nonassignable Clause, if not already part of policy contract.

III. Additional remarks:

Please mail the necessary forms and/or request for additional information to:

_____
(Agent's Name)

_____
(Agent's Address)

_____
(Policyowner's Signature)

Prepare Yourself

You can do several things to prepare for a successful total needs delivery interview:

1. think of additional services you can provide for clients;
2. look for additional insurance needs or problems that you can help the clients solve now or later;
3. prepare lists of prospects the clients may know and can help qualify and

4. make sure you're physically, mentally and psychologically ready for the delivery interview.

Record All Pertinent Information

In addition to the data provided on the policy records, you've developed a wealth of information about your new insureds—their situations, their families, their holdings, their attitudes, their priorities, their weaknesses, their goals and their dreams. Because all of this information may prove extremely valuable during future sales and service calls, retain it for future reference.

The Delivery Interview

A proper delivery interview is a very important part of the total needs selling process. It reassures your clients that they did the right thing. It gives them a better understanding of the plan, thereby creating a great sense of security and peace of mind. It also enables you to wind up a case with not only a satisfied client, but also a number of excellent prospects for additional sales and a stage properly set for repeat sales to the client. There is no better way to enhance the four vital "Ps" of our business: Production, Persistency, Profit and Prestige.

More is involved than merely delivering the plan summary and new insurance. A proper delivery interview fulfills three primary objectives.

Solidify Sale of Plan, New Insurance and Agent

You can accomplish the first part of this objective by presenting the plan summary and carefully reviewing everything in it. The second part involves making the insureds so pleased with their new policies that they want to keep them in force far into the future. The third part is accomplished by making the insureds so pleased with your professional service that they want to be your clients, not just insureds. This sets the stage for attaining the second and third objectives, which are the real business-builders.

Obtain New Prospects and Referrals

The second major objective in the delivery interview is to do good referred-lead prospecting and qualifying while the new clients are enthusiastic about their new total needs plan. This also is good for the new clients because if they truly are sold on their newly purchased plan—and on you—they can gain considerable enjoyment by sharing their good fortune with their friends.

A direct request for referrals is best. You might ask at the conclusion of the interview: "What other people do you know who might be interested in this service? Would you mind giving me a recommendation to them?" Obtaining a card or letter of introduction—or a personal face-to-face introduction—from clients is helpful. Many agents also prepare a list of potential prospects the new policyowners know. Having the list made up in advance makes it easier for clients to help provide leads and reminds you to ask for leads.

There's a well-known saying: "Behind every sale is a market much more valuable than the sale itself." A carefully planned delivery interview will open the door to that market, especially in total needs selling.

Create an Environment for the Next Purchase

The third major objective of a proper delivery interview is securing agreement from the client for you to review his or her situation in the near future in light of any changes that may occur, to render any service required and to discuss any additional insurance needs at that time. This phase of the delivery interview sets the stage for the next purchase sometime in the not too distant future and, hopefully, for repeat purchases over the years ahead.

■ CONTINUING SERVICE

Providing continuing service after a sale is important in all selling but it is especially important in total needs selling. The total needs sale should be only the beginning of many future sales. Moreover, you have a professional obligation to provide continuing service. We will turn now to when it should be provided.

Critical Premium Contact

After you have closed a total needs sale and made proper delivery, the most valuable thing you can do is to make a simple follow-up contact on the new clients at the next premium due date. This is the first time they have to send in a premium without you there to collect it and to remind them of what they are getting for it. The greatest number of lapses occur at this time. A small investment of your effort at this critical premium time can help to reassure clients that purchasing the policies was the right decision.

A phone call often is adequate. It should be an easy, natural call—possibly asking if the clients have any questions or how everything is going. During the delivery interview, you promised to keep in touch, so a call will come as no surprise.

The contact is important because it:

1. reminds the clients of the premium due, whether or not you specifically mention it;
2. reminds the clients of the plan, the insurance and your sincere interest in them and
3. gives the clients an opportunity to mention doubts while you can do something about them.

Application of the critical premium contact helps to keep business on the books. Besides, the interest you demonstrate binds new clients more securely to you.

Keep in Touch

You have established a wonderful relationship with your clients. They are happy with the plan and the insurance they've purchased. They want you to handle their personal insurance affairs hereafter.

If you want to preserve that relationship and enjoy all the rewards, your job doesn't end here. Your clients' personal and business situations change, including family status, home income and living standards, interests and objectives, insurance needs, friends, neighbors and associates. These changes create needs for service, opportunities for additional insurance sales and additional referred leads.

Keep in touch with your clients even if there is little hope of selling them again soon. Every contact need not be a business call. It might be a birthday card, a phoned word of congratulations, a note of sympathy or an introduction to a new customer. Each contact lets the clients know that you know and care.

Periodic Reviews

You should never let a year pass without making an appointment to review a client's situation and total needs plan. It might be at age change, policy anniversary or any other change that affects clients or their families. This should be a business call, much as the original sales and delivery interviews. Pay special attention to changes in the clients' situations that have occurred since the last review. Make appropriate changes in the plan, adding any additional insurance needed to satisfy current objectives. Clients normally appreciate this service.

This is another good time to ask for the names of others who might need similar service: your clients have met new people, made new friends and may even have new neighbors or business associates. Usually they'll be happy to tell you about such people.

Providing this kind of periodic review for clients is absolutely necessary. It's the key to retaining clients and expanding your clientele. There are few, if any, other ways that such a relatively small amount of time and effort can prove so rewarding in sales, persistence, goodwill, prestige and personal satisfaction.

■ TOTAL NEEDS SELLING AND YOU

You now have completed this text on the philosophy, methodology and practicality of the several methods of total needs selling. In the process, you've examined the application of these methods in both one-income and two-income family situations, learning about fact-finding, engineering the plan, the selling interview, service procedures in wrapping up the sale and obtaining prospects for new total needs sales.

So, if you're a newcomer to total needs selling . . . get started. If you're an old-timer who has neglected this activity recently . . . get back into it. Pick out a few really good prospects and go see them. Have some solid fact-finding sessions. Get immersed in your prospects' financial problems. After you've started, you'll have ample incentive to follow-through from there. And most important, each case that you complete will open doors to others.

The potential rewards of total needs selling—top-notch referrals, repeat sales, client-building, quality business—are worth the time and effort. You'll experience more of that personal satisfaction that comes from knowing that you truly have helped others. After all, that's what makes the career of life insurance selling genuinely worthwhile.

■ CHAPTER 8 QUESTIONS FOR REVIEW

1. For the policy to provide funds for final expenses, the secondary beneficiary should be the insured's:

   a. minor children.
   b. spouse.
   c. estate or executor.
   d. business partner.

2. The greatest number of policy lapses occur:

   a. a year or more into the plan when the client can no longer afford coverage.
   b. when the client changes his or her mind about the needs that prompted the purchase of the plan.
   c. when the agent is unable to resell the plan at policy delivery.
   d. when the next premium is due after the policies have been delivered and the plan is in place.

3. In a total needs sale, the beneficiary designation should be:

   a. irrevocable.
   b. made by the agent.
   c. revocable.
   d. considered relatively unimportant.

4. In a total needs plan, group insurance should be used for:

   a. cash funds.
   b. long-term needs.
   c. income needs.
   d. All of the above

5. Mentioning all possible alternatives in the selling interview:

   a. increases the chance of the sale because of the number of choices available.
   b. may lose the sale because the chance for indecision has been increased.
   c. impresses the prospect with the agent's technical knowledge.
   d. makes the sale inevitable.

⬛⬛⬛⬛⬛ Answer Key to Questions for Review

CHAPTER 1

1. b
2. d
3. c
4. c
5. b

CHAPTER 2

1. d
2. b
3. c
4. b
5. d

CHAPTER 3

1. c
2. b
3. b
4. c
5. d

CHAPTER 4

1. b
2. b
3. c
4. c
5. b

CHAPTER 5

1. a
2. a
3. c
4. a
5. b

CHAPTER 6

1. b
2. d
3. d
4. a
5. c

CHAPTER 7

1. a
2. a
3. c
4. b
5. a

CHAPTER 8

1. c
2. d
3. c
4. a
5. b

····· **Appendix**

■ **FACT-FINDING FORMS**

1. Essential Information
2. Objectives
3. Total Needs Work Sheet (side 1)
4. Total Needs Work Sheet (side 2)
5. Family Financial Summary
6. Recommendations and Key Benefits

ESSENTIAL INFORMATION

This is the first step in a personalized service designed to illustrate clearly the values of your life insurance and to make your life insurance serve you most effectively. The accuracy of this service depends on the exactness of the information given. All information will be held in strict confidence.

Date _____

FAMILY DATA

YOU

Your Name: _____ Birth Date: _____ Health: _____

Home Address: _____ Home Telephone: _____

Occupation: _____ Employer: _____

Business Address: _____ Business Telephone: _____

Do you and/or your spouse own an interest in the business? _____ Details: _____

_____

(If an answer is the same as above or not applicable, write "Same" or "N.A." respectively in the blank.)

YOUR SPOUSE

Spouse's Name: _____ Marriage Date: _____ Birth Date: _____ Health: _____

Home Address: _____ Home Telephone: _____

Occupation: _____ Employer: _____

Business Address: _____ Business Telephone: _____

Do you and/or your spouse own an interest in the business? _____ Details: _____

_____

YOUR CHILDREN AND/OR OTHER DEPENDENTS

Names	Relationships	Birth Date	Ages	Sex	Health	Other Information

FINANCIAL DATA

Amount

ANNUAL INCOME

Your Current Annual Earnings. . . . . $ _____

Intend to continue working for how long? _____ If your spouse should die? _____

Spouse's Current Annual Earnings . . . . $ _____

Intend to continue working for how long? _____ If you should die? _____

Annual Income From Other Sources (investments, trusts, etc.) . . . . $ _____

Total Current Annual Income . . . . $ _____

PRESENT GENERAL ASSETS

(List cash, checking and/or savings accounts, U.S. Savings Bonds, other bonds, stocks, mutual funds, residence, other real estate, business interests, vested pension or profit-sharing plans, personal property, other assets)

	Owner*	Approximate Current Liquidation Value	Approximate Current Annual Income
		$	$
Total Present Assets		$	$

*Owner: Y—You; S—Spouse; J—Joint; C—Community Property

PRESENT LIABILITIES

(List mortgage on residence, current bills, installment debts, notes, unpaid taxes, other indebtedness)

	Approximate Balance Owing	Approximate Payments
	$	$
Total Liabilities	$	$

PRESENT LIFE INSURANCE

(On You, Spouse, Children and Dependents, if applicable)

Person Insured	Company	Face Amount	Kind (Include additional benefits)	Issue Age	Policy Loan

GOVERNMENT BENEFITS DATA

**SOCIAL
SECURITY**
You: Covered? _____; How long?_____; % of Max. Earnings?_____; Soc. Sec. No. _____
Spouse: Covered?_____; How long? _____; % of Max. Earnings?_____; Soc. Sec. No. _____

MISCELLANEOUS DATA

WILLS
You: Have a will?_____; Date _____; When last revised?_____; Executor_____
Spouse: Have a will?_____; Date _____; When last revised?_____; Executor_____
Have you taken advantage of marital deduction privileges?_____; Named a guardian for minors?_____

(Give Name and Address if applicable)

Your: Attorney _____

**ADVISERS
BANKS**
Accountant _____
Bank _____
Spouse's: Attorney _____
Accountant _____
Bank _____

**TRUSTS —
BEQUESTS —
GIFTS — ETC.**
Are you or spouse involved in any trusts?_____; Any inheritances or bequests? _____; Made any gifts?_____
Pertinent data:_____
_____

**HEALTH
PLANS**
You: Disability Income $_____ for _____ years sickness or _____ years accident; Medical Expense_____
Spouse: Disability Income $_____ for_____ years sickness or _____ years accident; Medical Expense_____
Other details_____

**PENSION
PLANS**
You?_____; Est. income $_____ at age _____; Spouse? _____; Est. income $_____ at age_____
Other details_____

OTHER
Is there any other information that might be helpful in evaluating your situation?_____
_____

**LOCATION OF
IMPORTANT
ITEMS**
(Safety deposit box and key, bank accounts, marriage license, birth certificates, will, other vital papers, etc.)_____
_____
_____

FAMILY FINANCIAL OBJECTIVES

	If You Die	If Spouse Dies		If You Die	If Spouse Dies
Monthly bills, total _____	$ _____	$ _____	Death taxes:		
*Installment purchases _____	$ _____	$ _____	Federal _____	$ _____	$ _____
*Loans _____	$ _____	$ _____	State _____	$ _____	$ _____
Doctors, hospital, nurses, funeral _____	$ _____	$ _____	Emergency fund _____	$ _____	$ _____
			**Bequests _____	$ _____	$ _____
Legal fees, court costs, executor's fee and bond _____	$ _____	$ _____	Other _____	$ _____	$ _____
*Current unpaid taxes _____	$ _____	$ _____	Total Final Expense Fund Needs	$ _____	$ _____

FINAL EXPENSE FUND NEEDS

*See Page 2   **See Page 3

HOUSING FUND NEED

	If You Die	If Spouse Dies
Continuation of mortgage payments of ____ $_____ a month for _____ years	$_____ a month for _____ years	
Or, liquidation of mortgage with _____ Cash of $ _____	Cash of $_____	
Or, rental payments of _____ $ _____ a month for _____ years	$ _____ a month for _____ years	
Other arrangement _____	_____	_____

EDUCATION FUND NEEDS

For (Child):				
If You Die	$	$	$	$
If Spouse Dies	$	$	$	$

MONTHLY INCOME NEEDS

	If You Die	If Spouse Dies		If You Die	If Spouse Dies
Food _____	$ _____	$ _____	Medical and dental care _____	$ _____	$ _____
Clothing (inc. laundry and cleaning)	$ _____	$ _____	Housing payment, if any _____	$ _____	$ _____
Utilities (incl. heat) _____	$ _____	$ _____	Miscellaneous _____	$ _____	$ _____
Home maintenance _____	$ _____	$ _____	Other _____	$ _____	$ _____
Property taxes _____	$ _____	$ _____	Total Immediate Monthly Family Income Needs _____	$ _____	$ _____
Transportation _____	$ _____	$ _____			

TOTAL NEEDS SUMMARY AND PRIORITIES

NEEDS	If YOU Should Die	Order of Priority	If Your SPOUSE Dies	Order of Priority	If You BOTH Live
CASH:					
Final Expense Fund	$_____	( )	$_____	( )	
Housing Fund (Lump sum, if any)	$_____	( )	$_____	( )	
Education Fund	$_____	( )	$_____	( )	
INCOME:					
Children's Dependency Period —					
While more than 1 child under age 18	$_____	( )	$_____	( )	
While only 1 child under age 18	$_____	( )	$_____	( )	
Spouse's Life Income — to age _____	$_____	( )			
— For life thereafter	$_____	( )			
Your Life Income — to age _____			$_____	( )	
— For life thereafter			$_____	( )	
RETIREMENT INCOME: At your age_____					$_____

ADDITIONAL OBJECTIVES (needs and desires): _____

FUNDING   If needed to accomplish the above objectives, how much additional could you set aside? $_____ per _____

OBJECTIVES

Objectives	If Husband Dies	If Wife Dies

Cash Needs:

Final Expenses
Housing Fund
Education Fund

Monthly Income Needs:

Dependency Period Income:
Until _____ is age 18
Until _____ is age 16
Until _____ is age 18

Spouse's Life Income:
To Wife to age 65
For life thereafter

To Husband to age 65
For life thereafter

Retirement income at _____ age _____ if both live

TOTAL NEEDS WORK SHEET

CASH NEEDS

If _____ Dies (Husband)   If _____ Dies (Wife)

	Objectives	S.S. and/or Other Govt. Benefits	Present Requirements	Objectives	S.S. and/or Other Govt. Benefits	Present Requirements
Final Expenses	$	$	$	$	$	$
Housing Fund						
Education Fund						

TOTAL CASH NEEDS $ _____   TOTAL CASH NEEDS $ _____

MONTHLY INCOME NEEDS

If _____ Dies (Husband)   _____'s Age (Wife)

☐ ☐ ☐ ☐ ☐ Life

	For __ Depend. Yrs. While 3 or More Elig.	For __ Depend. Yrs. While 2 Eligible	For __ Depend. Yrs. While 1 Eligible	For __ Yrs. Until Wife is Age __	Wife for Life
Objectives	$	$	$	$	$
S. S. and/or Other Govt. Benefits					
Continuing Income (Wife)					
Present Requirements	$	$	$	$	$
	$	$	$	$	$

Capital Amounts
$ _____
_____
_____
_____
_____
$ _____

If _____ Dies (Wife)   _____'s Age (Husband)

☐ ☐ ☐ ☐ ☐ Life

	For __ Depend. Yrs. While 3 or More Elig.	For __ Depend. Yrs. While 2 Eligible	For __ Depend. Yrs. While 1 Eligible	For __ Yrs. Until Husband is Age __	Husband for Life
Objectives	$	$	$	$	$
S. S. and/or Other Govt. Benefits					
Continuing Income (Husband)					
Present Requirements	$	$	$	$	$
	$	$	$	$	$

Capital Amounts
$ _____
_____
_____
_____
_____
$ _____

TOTAL PRESENT REQUIREMENTS

If _____ Dies $ _____ (Husband)   If _____ Dies $ _____ (Wife)

Side 1

PRESENT REQUIREMENTS vs. PRESENT RESOURCES

If _____ Dies If _____ Dies
(Husband)   (Wife)

Total Present Capital Requirements $_____ $_____

Present Life Insurance Applicable $_____ $_____

Other Present Asset Values Applicable $_____ $_____

Total Present Capital Resources $_____ $_____

New Life Insurance Required $_____ $_____

NEW INSURANCE RECOMMENDED

On _____ $_____ _____ $_____/_____
(Husband)   (Amount) (Policy or Combination of Policies)   (Premium)

On _____ $_____ _____ $_____/_____
(Wife)   (Amount) (Policy or Combination of Policies)   (Premium)

LIVING VALUES

RETIREMENT INCOME

For _____ at _____ AND _____ at _____ — _____
(Husband)   (age)   (Wife)   (age)   (year)

Monthly
Life Income

From:

Social Security and/or Other Gov't Benefits   _____ $_____
                                                (Husband)
                                                _____
                                                (Wife)

Pension and/or Profit Sharing Plans   _____   _____
                                        (Husband)
                                        _____
                                        (Wife)   Option or
                                                   Earnings Rate

Present Life Insurance   _____   (_____)   _____
                          (Husband)
                          _____   (_____)   _____
                          (Wife)

New Life Insurance   _____   (_____)   _____
                      (Husband)
                      _____   (_____)   _____
                      (Wife)

Other   _____   _____

         _____   _____

Total Monthly Retirement Income $_____

MISCELLANEOUS (Education, Opportunity, Emergency Funds, etc.)

Side 2

PREPARED FOR:_____   DATE:_____

FAMILY FINANCIAL SUMMARY

	For _____ if (Wife) _____ should die. (Husband)	For _____ if (Husband) _____ should die. (Wife)
CASH NEEDS		
Final Expenses – Objective	$_____	$_____
Less Social Security and/or Other Benefits	$_____	$_____
Present Requirement	$_____	$_____
Your Housing Fund – Present Requirement	$_____	$_____
Your Children's Education – Objective	$_____	$_____
Less Social Security and/or Other Benefits	$_____	$_____
Present Requirement	$_____	$_____
Total Cash Needs	$_____	$_____
MONTHLY INCOME NEEDS		
Dependency Period – 3 or more eligible – Objective	$_____	$_____
Less Social Security and/or Other Benefits	$_____	$_____
Less Continuing Personal Income	$_____	$_____
Present Requirement (Income–Capital)	$_____ – $_____	$_____ – $_____
Dependency Period – 2 eligible – Objective	$_____	$_____
Less Social Security and/or Other Benefits	$_____	$_____
Less Continuing Personal Income	$_____	$_____
Present Requirement (Income–Capital)	$_____ – $_____	$_____ – $_____
Dependency Period – 1 eligible – Objective	$_____	$_____
Less Social Security and/or Other Benefits	$_____	$_____
Less Continuing Personal Income	$_____	$_____
Present Requirement (Income–Capital)	$_____ – $_____	$_____ – $_____
For spouse (no children) – Objective	$_____	$_____
– to Age	_____	_____
Less Continuing Personal Income	$_____	$_____
Present Requirement (Income–Capital)	$_____ – $_____	$_____ – $_____
For spouse (no children) – Objective	$_____	$_____
– for Life After Age	_____	_____
Less Social Security and/or Other Benefits	$_____	$_____
Less Continuing Personal Income	$_____	$_____
Present Requirement (Income–Capital)	$_____ – $_____	$_____ – $_____
Total Capital to Satisfy Income Needs	$_____	$_____
Total Capital to Satisfy Cash and Income Needs	$_____	$_____
Less Existing Life Insurance and Other Assets	$_____	$_____
Amount Still Required to Satisfy Your Objectives	$_____	$_____

RECOMMENDATIONS:

RETIREMENT INCOME if you live, starting at _____ 's age _____ and _____ 's age _____:
(Husband)   (Wife)

From Social Security and/or Other Government Benefit Plans .... $_____

From Present Insurance, Employee Retirement Plans, and Other Resources .... $_____

From Recommended New Life Insurance .... $_____

Total Retirement Income .... $_____

RECOMMENDATIONS AND KEY BENEFITS

A. POLICY RECOMMENDATIONS

To provide the additional capital required to satisfy your family financial objectives completely if either of you should not live, it is recommended that you purchase additional life insurance as follows:

On _____ life:
           (husband's)

    Whole Life _____ :   at _____ per mo
    Other _____ :   at _____ per mo
    _____ :   _____ per mo

On _____ life:
           (wife's)

    Whole Life _____ :   at _____ per mo
    Other _____ :   at _____ per mo
    _____ :   _____ per mo

B. RETIREMENT INCOME

If the recommended program is adopted, your monthly retirement income at _____ age 65 and _____ age 65 will be as follows: (husband's)
(wife's)

From _____ (husband's)	Social Security	$ _____
From _____ (husband's)	present insurance and pension	$ _____
From _____ (husband's)	recommended new life insurance	$ _____
From _____ (wife's)	Social Security	$ _____
From _____ (wife's)	recommended new life insurance	$ _____
From _____ (wife's)	present insurance and pension	$ _____
From other liquid assets		$ _____
Total Monthly Retirement Income		$ _____

C. EDUCATION FUNDS

The recommended program will make education funds available as follows:

	At age 18	*At age 18*
From loans on present insurance		
From loans on new insurance		
From other liquid assets (estimate)		
Total Funds Available		

D. EARLY CAPITAL GIFT POSSIBILITY

In the unfortunate event of _____ early death, a surplus of capital required to
(husband's)
satisfy your objectives would arise after your youngest child attains age 18. Accordingly, if desired, the following early capital gift could be made without shortening your stated objectives:

■ **NOTES**

■ **NOTES**

■ NOTES

■ NOTES

■ **NOTES**